Shakespeare's Playhouse Practice

The University Press
of New England

Sponsoring Institutions

Brandeis University
Clark University
Dartmouth College
The University of New Hampshire
The University of Rhode Island
The University of Vermont

Shakespeare's Playhouse Practice

A HANDBOOK

Warren D. Smith

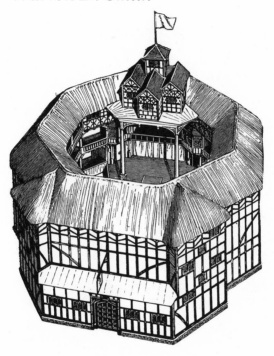

Published for the University of Rhode Island
by the University Press of New England
Hanover, New Hampshire 1975

TO BETTY

Contents

Preface

☞ It has long been recognized that the physical aspects of the Elizabethan public playhouse, as well as the nature of the contemporary audience, influenced the composition of Shakespeare's plays. But readers, students, teachers, actors, and directors with inquiring minds might well want, possibly need, to learn the specific nature of the playhouse conventions the dramatist adopted in adjusting his craft to the physical aspects of the theater if not to the particular audience for which he wrote. Therefore I have attempted, within the smallest possible compass, to present what is intended to be used, primarily at least, as a handbook supplementary to the study, in or out of the classroom, of Shakespeare's plays as great literary drama: to gather together in a manual readily accessible to everyone satisfactory answers to theatrical questions that occur from time to time to alert readers and participants in the theater—why, for instance, does Shakespeare, unlike the modern dramatist, so often have a character greet the entrance of a newcomer to the scene with undramatic statements like "Here he comes," or "Look where he comes." Most students and all theater personnel, including writers for arena or radio productions, should be interested in discovering what obliged the dramatist, in contrast to modern practice, to insert ten times as many directions for stage business into his dialogue as appear in the marginal notations of the basic texts. If "aloft" was originally supposed to designate the balcony stage, as editors of the plays have assumed it did, how is it that the playwright allows only from one to three lines of dialogue, far less than the time required, for some of the ascents and descents in the plays? Much has been written about the monologues, but there have been no answers to questions like how does the apostrophe differ from the soliloquy and the aside, or, are there really only two types of asides (only four asides of any kind are marked in the First Folio) in the drama of Shakespeare? Also the reader might readily be puzzled, as any thoughtful theater director is bound to be, by the fact that there are so many unspecific references in the old drama to the outdoors, and to external features of interiors. Moreover, writing for a roofless, open-air playhouse and for performances produced in broad daylight—with the sky above as the only lighting for the stage—why does the dramatist give so many references to "morning," as well as to, what is more understandable under the circumstances, "night"? Finally, what could possibly have induced Shakespeare, again unlike the modern dramatist, to mark almost every exit in all the plays with what are evidently cues to the actors (there were no actresses) to leave the stage at the appropriate moment?

To demonstrate clearly how and why Shakespeare employed each device in his dialogue demands a liberal sprinkling of quotations from the plays, a method that has the advantage of permitting the dramatist himself to reveal his practice directly, so to speak, to the reader of the handbook. A similarly happy result, I venture to hope, has been reached by the avoidance of citations from secondary sources, which also has rendered the addition of a bibliography unnecessary, though, it goes without saying, I am deeply indebted to a host of fellow commentators in allied studies, as I am thankful for my own experience as actor and director as well as long-time instructor and researcher in Shakespeare.

Also for the convenience of the reader I have modernized (according to Kittredge) the spelling and punctuation, except for the marginal notations in the basic texts, of all quotations, though only after having consulted the initial authentic printing of the play, carefully checking each pre-1623 quarto against the First Folio, and taking into account significant variations. Thus the quotations, though modernized, were originally taken from the "good" quarto, if there was one, or from the First Folio, if that presented the earliest reliable text. The Folio text was chosen as basic for *Richard III* and *King Lear* because the authenticity of the quartos of both plays remains dubious. On the other hand, personal eccentricity (rather than an attempt to achieve authenticity) is responsible for the British spelling, with the *r* before the *e*, in the title *Globe Theatre,* whenever it appears, in contrast to the American spelling, *theater,* whenever the term is used generally throughout the rest of the text. And to avoid entering the controversy in terminology that has been alive during the past two decades concerning the old designation "inner stage" as opposed to the more modern "discovery space" or the like—a controversy which, though of no little importance in itself, is not relevant to the purpose of this handbook—I have adopted the more neutral term "inner space" to represent the playing area, with a curtain, somewhere upstage of the main platform.

Because of the controversial opinions that continue to be expressed about Shakespeare's share in the composing of *Pericles* and *Henry VIII,* I have omitted both. If the dramatist wrote 60 percent or so of *Pericles,* it would still be impossible to disentangle his

Preface

stagecraft from that of a collaborator; and in *Henry VIII* the great part of playhouse practice to be found is likely Fletcher's. On the other hand, I include the three *Henry VI* plays because of the opinion generally held that Shakespeare at least revised them, and therefore presumably approved, if he did not alter, the stagecraft therein.

One word more: my gratitude still goes to Professors Matthew Black and Mathais Shaaber, who more than a quarter of a century ago helped steer my course through a doctoral dissertation at the University of Pennsylvania, which finally, as it turned out, proved to be the germ of this study of Shakespeare's craftsmanship.

Kingston, R.I.   W. D. S.
July 1974

Shakespeare's Playhouse Practice

ONE

Entrance Announcements

☞ Every reader has noticed that for many entrances to an occupied stage[1] Shakespeare, often with dramatic effectiveness, has an occupant announce the approach of a newcomer by stating: "Here he comes," "Look where he comes," or the like.[2] It has not been demonstrated how admirably the convention—discarded, not unnaturally, by the modern dramatist—is fitted to certain physical peculiarities of the Elizabethan stage.[3]

The immediate function of the device was to inform the audience that the attention of characters on the stage was being directed to the enterers, in order to give these onstage characters the excuse necessary to shift their positions in preparation for a graceful regrouping.[4] No more than modern actors would

1. I count 450 entrance announcements in Shakespeare. The 718 entrances to a cleared stage at the beginnings of scenes of course offer no opportunity for the use of the device.

2. That such lines are not for the identification of enterers is shown by the fact that the great majority of announcements do not include the name of the enterer.

3. An examination of European, British, and American plays from Ibsen to the present reveals only widely scattered, incidental examples of anything resembling the Elizabethan entrance announcement.

4. Though the entrance announcement must have helped to draw the attention of the audience, as well, it was not needed for this function, as is demonstrated by the fact that fully 203 enterers draw attention to themselves by speaking immediately after the announcement of their entrance.

Shakespeare's Playhouse Practice

Elizabethan players on the stage at the time of an entrance need the announcement as a cue for what to do next. But whenever a stage occupant, Elizabethan or modern, is supposed to change his position because of the entrance of a newcomer, such a movement should be tied in with the entrance as smoothly as possible. And because of physical aspects peculiar to the Elizabethan public stage, the entrance announcement seems to have been one of the few appropriate methods by which Shakespeare could inform his audience that stage occupants were fully aware of the enterer's approach and that it was this awareness which precipitated their stage movement. Either by making such an announcement himself or by receiving the word from a fellow player, frequently the actor on Shakespeare's stage gives his audience the necessary justification for his movement before the enterer has the chance to speak, to be greeted by one of the occupants, or to enter the stage picture.[5] To anyone unfamiliar with theater practice, it might seem that the opening line of the enterer who is to speak immediately after the announcement of his entrance would provide such justification, but speech from the newcomer would more often than not come too late to be practicable. For example, in Shakespeare as in modern plays, exits precipitated by impending entrances[6] and withdrawals to hiding places for the purpose of eavesdropping on the newcomers[7] obviously must be completed before enterers reach the stage. And the overwhelming majority of the entrance announcements in

5. In 59 cases the announcer himself greets the newcomer immediately after his entrance, and in 43 instances the recipient of the announcement greets the enterer instantly.

6. See *Love's Labour's Lost,* V.ii.308–309; *Romeo and Juliet,* I.i.163; and *Measure for Measure,* IV.i.7–9.

7. See *Richard II,* III.iv.24–28; *Much Ado About Nothing,* II.iii.36–38; and *Hamlet,* III.iv.7.

Entrance Announcements

Shakespeare's plays (429 of 450) prepare the stage for a regrouping that will include both occupants and enterers, and should therefore be delivered some time before the entrance is completed. An illustration from *Titus Andronicus* is instructive:

> *Captain.* Romans, make way. The good
> Andronicus. . . .   (I.i.64)

followed, in the quarto, by the unusually full notation

> . . . *enter two of Titus' sons, and then two men bearing a coffin . . . then two other sons; then Titus Andronicus; and then Tamora, . . . and her two sons, . . . with Aaron the Moor and others, as many as can be . . .*

—a notation presenting sufficient reason for the captain's request of his fellow Romans to "make way." Both the captain and his companions could well use some kind of warning beforehand to shift their positions fast enough to prepare the stage for the graceful entrance of so many characters. And the entrance announcement "The good Andronicus" adequately motivates the captain's giving such a warning in good time. Of similar nature is an announcement made in *Much Ado About Nothing* (II.i.87–88), by Leonato to Antonio and the other members of his family on the stage with him:

> The revellers are ent'ring, brother. Make good
> room,

succeeded by the stage direction

> *Enter Don Pedro, Claudio, Benedick, and Balthasar, Don John,*

because the notation in the quarto at the beginning of the scene indicates at least five characters already on the stage when this entrance of five more is accomplished.[8] Thus Leonato's advice to "make good room" precedes the entrance of the revelers so that they may join the stage grouping with a minimum of awkward, belated shifting on the part of Leonato and his family. And, as in the previous example quoted from *Titus Andronicus,* Shakespeare motivates Leonato's timely advice with an announcement, "The revellers are ent'ring." And for similar motivation, though with less obvious wording, the entrance announcement is used abundantly in the plays of Shakespeare's contemporaries, as well as in his own.[9]

But why was the entrance announcement, seldom if ever used by modern dramatists,[10] habitually em-

8. The entrance notation in the 1600 quarto of *Much Ado About Nothing* adds "his wife," the mute Innogen.

9. Elizabethan plays (other than Shakespeare's) with more than a dozen entrance announcements are, for example, Peele's *Old Wives Tale,* Greene and Lodge's *Looking-Glass,* Marlowe's *Jew of Malta* and *Edward II,* Chapman's *All Fools* and *Gentleman Usher,* Dekker's *Honest Whore Part I,* and Jonson's *Every Man in His Humour, Every Man Out of His Humour* (at least 32 entrance announcements), and *Bartholomew Fair.* Indeed, there would seem to be few if any leading plays from Marlowe to the closing of the theaters without entrance announcements.

10. It is perhaps interesting to note that the entrance announcement begins to fall into disuse immediately after the Restoration, with the advent of the proscenium arch. For example, Otway's *Venice Preserved* has only a few scattered instances, and neither Dryden and Howard's *Indian Queen* nor Buckingham's *Rehearsal* has any. On the other hand, many of the Restoration plays (Etherege's *Man of Mode,* Lee's *Rival Queens,* and Dryden's *All for Love*) employ the entrance announcement regularly. That the convention should have persisted after the introduction of the proscenium arch was rather puzzling until I remembered that a considerable apron, along with the old doors, survived long after the Restoration, bearing a closer resemblance to the Elizabethan platform than to the modern picture-frame stage.

ployed by Shakespeare, along with his contemporaries? The answer depends, dramaturgically at least,[11] upon the vast difference between the modern shallow stage, framed by a proscenium arch, and the Elizabethan outer platform, projecting deeply into the pit of the public playhouse. What justified Shakespeare's entrance announcement, often extradramatically, I believe, were two characteristics peculiar to the Elizabethan outer platform stage: its great depth (twenty-nine feet, nearly twice that of many modern stages) and, in the absence of a proscenium arch, the extreme upstage position of its two main entranceways.

That Shakespeare's employment of the entrance announcement, even undramatically, was made appropriate by these important physical aspects of his outer platform is most clearly illustrated by a rather obtrusive example from an early play, *The Two Gentlemen of Verona.* In this instance the player who announces the entrance stands alone on the stage. As "Proteus" he is telling the audience how infatuated he has permitted himself to become with "Silvia." Then he abruptly breaks off his soliloquy with these undramatic lines:

> . . . But here comes Thurio. Now must we to her window
> And give some evening music to her ear.
> (IV.ii.16–17)

and as soon as Thurio and the musicians with him have

---

11. Although, as with any convention he adopts, Shakespeare frequently utilizes the entrance announcement to heighten the dramatic effectiveness of a situation, I have confined myself throughout this work to the usefulness of the device purely from the standpoint of stagecraft. It must be admitted that many, if not most, of Shakespeare's entrance announcements are not dramatically impressive.

completed their entrance, this is exactly what is done. But why does the dramatist have Proteus announce the entrance? Why not, as in a modern play, let him reveal he sees the approach of Thurio by having him join the newcomer under Silvia's "window" without preliminary explanation? For one thing, more than likely the actor in the part delivered his soliloquy, on the remarkably deep Elizabethan platform, from pretty far downstage, certainly with the extreme upstage entranceways some distance to his rear. That a performer could be in such intimate touch with the majority of his audience was the great advantage of the public stage for the rendering of soliloquies. Also, it is generally accepted that the "window" to which Thurio, as well as Proteus, goes immediately after the entrance was at the extreme rear of the Elizabethan platform—was, in fact, part of the front wall of the second level of the tiring house. Thus the entrance announcement "here comes Thurio" neatly gives Proteus the opportunity to assure his audience that he is aware of the presence of a newcomer who enters behind him and who goes to another location (under Silvia's window) behind him. Without the announcement, as Proteus turns away and walks upstage to join Thurio under Silvia's window, spectators would be left to puzzle out for themselves how, while facing front for his soliloquy, Proteus saw the enterers at his back. Actually, Proteus would be equally blind to the approach whether or not he made an entrance announcement, but the artifice would induce the audience to overlook the fact.

Far more natural, in contrast, is an example in *A Midsummer Night's Dream* (II.i.58–59) where two players on the stage warn each other in turn to move before each of two separate entrances:

> *Puck.* . . . But room, fairy! Here comes
>   Oberon.
> *Fairy.* And here my mistress. . . .

followed by a stage direction—

> *Enter the King of Fairies, at one door, with
> his Train; and the Queen, at another, with
> hers,*

which discloses that Oberon and Titania enter through
two different doors. What occurs seems fairly easy to
picture. Facing in the general direction of the door
(though downstage from it) through which Oberon
enters, Puck at once signals the audience he notices
the approach and gives the fairy—who with his back
turned toward the door cannot be expected by the audience to see Oberon—the excuse to move for the
King's entrance. In his turn, the fairy reveals his own
awareness of Titania's approach through the door on
the opposite side of the stage and at the same time
warns Puck—who with his back to that door cannot
see her—to prepare for the Queen's entrance. Puck's
"But room, fairy!" might indicate, of course, that at
least one of the stage occupants was standing directly
in the pathway of enterers and therefore had to scam-
per out of the way to avoid collision. But whatever
the result of the two announcements, I believe they
are primarily justified by the fact that each stage occupant, standing, like Proteus, with his back to one of
the entranceways, could not readily be assumed by
the audience to see the approach of newcomers behind him. Unlike Proteus, who must have faced front
for his soliloquy, however, Puck and the fairy, because
they must have at least partly faced each other for
their dialogue, could each be imagined to detect an entrance through the door toward which he was turned.

Shakespeare's Playhouse Practice

That players standing any distance downstage on Shakespeare's deep Elizabethan platform, with backs turned to the upstage entranceways, could not easily be assumed by spectators to see the approach of enterers seems also to be one of the reasons for those instances (seventy-nine in the plays) in which one stage occupant announces to another: "Look where he comes," "See where he comes," or the like. Only six plays[12] omit the "look where" type. In all these entrance announcements, though some admittedly are dramatically effective, what takes place is evident. As Puck and the fairy must have done, two actors stand on the deep platform stage, each with his back toward one of the upstage entranceways. A third player enters, or is about to enter. The one who faces in the general direction of the door through which the newcomer is making his entrance, and who thereby can be assumed by the audience to detect it visually (if only out of the corner of his eye), tells the other player with him to turn around and look in that direction. What better excuse to spectators could the actor with his back to the entranceway offer for abruptly turning away from the man with whom he has been conversing than the fact that this very person tells him to?

The modern actor, on the other hand, performing on a picture-frame stage little more than fifteen feet deep from the front curtain line to the rear, often with entranceways downstage, need utilize no such dramaturgical motivation for stage movement. In the first place, the proscenium arch and the apron before it combine to make the modern stage appear to be more shallow than it actually is. And the pertinent fact that all the members of a modern audience nor-

12. *Richard III, Richard II, The Merchant of Venice, 1 Henry IV, Henry V,* and *Coriolanus.*

mally view a play only from the front of the stage
rather than from three sides of it, as Elizabethans in
the public playhouses did, markedly increases the effect of shallowness. Hence, whenever the action demands it, a present day actor can be located almost
anywhere on the stage and still seem—from the view-
point of the audience out front—to be capable of seeing out of the corner of his eye the player who is making his entrance. I have sometimes directed an actor
to greet immediately another who is entering at a
point fully ten feet upstage from his own position. The
picture-frame illusion makes this look natural, even
from a seat at one of the extreme sides of the theater.
Such awareness of an entrance is not as acceptable, of
course, if the newcomer enters from upstage dead center, or if the stage occupant stands with his back to a
downstage entrance. But in these instances the actor
is frequently given the excuse to turn around and
greet the newcomer naturally (if he is supposed to do
so) by means of a "door slam" offstage catching his
auditory attention or a maid who flatly announces his
arrival. There is no evidence that either Shakespeare's
Theatre or Globe used door slams, and scenes where a
domestic servant is the appropriate announcer of an
entrance are few in the old drama. Yet, significantly
enough, Shakespeare did employ, whenever he could
do so fittingly, a device similar to the former of these
modern ones to offer some of his players on the stage
an excuse to give ground for the entrance of others.
Instead of the modern door slam, "A Sennet," "Sound
a Trumpet," "Flourish," and the like provide the offstage signal for numerous Shakespearean entrances,
whenever such sound effects are in keeping with the
rank of the approaching newcomers. Moreover, of the
450 announcements of all types in the plays, only

eight[13] are delivered in addition to sound effects, demonstrating an admirable economy in usage.

It may be of interest to note also that for those entrances which evidence in the text seems to establish as having occurred on an already occupied inner space,[14] Shakespeare normally omits the entrance announcement. Such entrances should not have presented the problem posed by the outer platform, where occupants often must have found themselves some distance downstage from the entranceway. The shallowness of both inner spaces, which according to the most reliable commentators were probably only seven or eight feet deep from curtain line to rear arras, would have obviated dramaturgical need for the entrance signal. For players occupying an inner space during an entrance were doubtless in a similar situation to players on the modern picture-frame stage:[15] they readily could have convinced the spectators of their ability to detect the approach of newcomers from the corners of their eyes, thereby justifying any stage movement necessary for them to make before the completion of the entrance. So that of the fourteen entrances in the two *Henry IV* plays to the al-

13. *2 Henry VI*, IV.viii.3–5; *Richard III*, IV.iv.135; *As You Like It*, I.ii.156–157; *Hamlet*, III.ii.95–96; *All's Well That Ends Well*, III.v.78; *King Lear*, I.i.34; *Antony and Cleopatra*, I.i.10 (the only "look where" type); and *Coriolanus*, II.ii.40.

14. Where the enterer appears on the balcony with the occupants on the lower, outer platform (for example, *Romeo and Juliet*, II.ii.2 and *Richard II*, III.iii.62), the case, of course, is altogether different.

15. The Elizabethan inner space had what must have amounted to a proscenium arch. Also, it will be remembered that through a gradual evolution the inner space of that time has now become our main stage and the Elizabethan outer platform, our apron—the space from the front curtain line to the footlights—before it fell into general disuse.

ready occupied "tavern" (which the furniture and dialogue[16] seem to establish as one of the inner spaces),
but one[17] is preceded by an entrance announcement.
And in the dramatist's other plays entrances which
the presence of furnishings and the situation seem to
reveal as having taken place on one of the two inner
spaces[18] go unannounced.

The evidence, then, indicates clearly that the convention of the entrance announcement, long since out-
moded, as purely a stagecraft device was, in the plays
of Shakespeare, beautifully fitted to the physical peculiarities of the outer platform stage of the public
playhouse for which he wrote.

16. For example, at *1 Henry IV*, II.iv.576, Peto notes that
Falstaff is fast asleep "behind the arras," a location at the rear
of the inner space; and at *2 Henry IV*, II.iv.74, a drawer announces that Ancient Pistol is "below," which could mean
that the tavern is really the upper inner space, or chamber, in
the balcony.

17. *1 Henry IV*, II.iv.358.

18. See, for example, *Richard III*, V.iii.207 (Ratcliff enters
Richard's tent); *The Merchant of Venice*, II.v.9 (Jessica enters
a room in Shylock's house, evidently the balcony stage because
afterward she re-enters above, to be serenaded by Lorenzo);
Othello, IV.ii.23, 92, and 109 (Emilia and Desdemona, Emilia
alone, and Emilia and Iago, respectively, enter Desdemona's
bedchamber); and *Coriolanus*, IV.v.4 (Coriolanus enters Aufidius' "house" after having asked a citizen where it is located).

TWO

Stage Business in the Dialogue

☞ In marked contrast to modern drama, Shake-speare's plays contain nearly three thousand directions for stage business (action performed without shifting position) in the dialogue[1] compared to three hundred and twenty marginal notations[2] in the basic texts. Most of these are spoken too late[3] to have served as instructions for the actors, and many that precede the action are impractical as cues because instead of helping the recipients, they place additional demands upon them.[4] Yet once we picture the

1. By plays, the number ranges from 35 in *Timon of Athens* to 138 in *Julius Caesar*, with no significant fluctuation in frequency according to period.

2. Some modern producers have found the directions in the dialogue to be far more helpful than the marginal notations.

3. Of the 2923 directions I count in the plays, fewer than 880 actually precede the action to which they allude. Furthermore, much stage business and practically all stage movement is performed without any accompanying verbal description (for an explanation, see below, pp. 20–22).

4. For example, Tybalt's challenge to Romeo, "turn and draw" (III.i.70) must assume that the actor in the part of Romeo has remembered (without the help of a cue) to face the other way before Tybalt delivers it (see also *Macbeth*, V.viii.3 and *The Winter's Tale*, V.iii.120). Likewise, in *Richard II* (III.ii.87), Aumerle, Carlisle, Salisbury, and some soldiers must remember (without a cue) to bow their heads preceding Richard's, "Look not to the ground." Even more impractical as cues are directions that are repeated because the recipients delay performing them, since a player cannot be expected to ignore the first "cue" and act only after he has received a second or third.

Shakespeare's Playhouse Practice

Elizabethan performance as viewed from three sides of the projecting platform, rather than from out front as in modern theaters, the practical stagecraft underlying the preponderance of directions in the dialogue readily emerges from artistic concealment. Just as italicized notations in the texts of modern drama are often descriptions of gestures for the benefit of the reader (who, of course, cannot otherwise perceive the action), so, I am convinced, Shakespeare's directions in the dialogue, along with those of his contemporaries,[5] are actually descriptions for spectators who could not be expected at the moment to see clearly the action on the stage of the Elizabethan public playhouse. Some members of an audience that surrounded three sides of the stage normally must have been blocked from seeing stage business either by the back of the performer or by the bodies of one or more intervening players. A vital function of the dramatist's dialogue descriptions, then, was to supply the information required whenever some important action was

5. Almost as consistent as Shakespeare's plays in the use of descriptions of stage business, for example, are Kyd's *Spanish Tragedy*, Jonson's *Every Man in His Humour*, Chapman's *Gentleman Usher*, and Massinger's *Maid of Honor*. I have also been struck by the regular occurrence of the device in Peele's *Arraignment of Paris, David and Bethsabe,* and *Old Wives Tale;* Greene's *Orlando Furioso* and *Friar Bacon;* Marlowe's *Tamburlaine* and *Edward II;* Dekker's *Shoemaker's Holiday, Old Fortunatus,* and *Honest Whore;* Heywood's *Woman Killed with Kindness, Wise Woman,* and *Fair Maid;* Jonson's *Every Man Out of His Humour, Sejanus, Volpone, Alchemist,* and *Bartholomew Fair;* Middleton's *Trick to Catch the Old One* and *Michaelmas Term;* Beaumont and Fletcher's *Philaster, Maid's Tragedy,* and *King and No King;* Massinger's *New Way to Pay Old Debts;* and Ford's *Love's Sacrifice, 'Tis Pity She's a Whore, Broken Heart,* and *Perkin Warbeck.* Indeed, the convention seems to permeate the whole era, appearing in at least as early a play as *Cambises* and in as late a one as Brome's *Jovial Crew.*

masked from part of the audience by the back of a
player or by the intervening body of another on the
Elizabethan three-sided public stage.

That this was the case is demonstrated in Shakespeare's consistent practice of naming stage properties[6]
large enough and distinctive enough[7] to be seen and
identified from any part of a modern theater. Even so
unobtrusive an example as Macbeth's dramatically appropriate outcry to the three witches, "Why sinks that
cauldron?" (*Macbeth,* IV.i.106), includes the practical
function of informing those spectators who could not
see it easily at the moment that this property was
about to disappear, probably through a trapdoor. For
on the Elizabethan platform stage, unless Macbeth and
the three witches placed themselves at the extreme
rear against the tiring-house wall, with the cauldron
well in front of them (an unlikely grouping), one or
more of the actors would have at least partly masked
the cauldron, sizable as it was, from the view of some
members of the audience. A kettle either to one side
of all four players or between them would have been
obstructed from the vision of spectators located at
one of the sides of the projecting platform (at least at
eye level). And if the group stood downstage (at the
front of the platform) with the cauldron in front of
them, spectators located in positions upstage from
them would have difficulty seeing it. Thus Macbeth
refers specifically to the sinking cauldron—in part,
at least—for the benefit of members of his audience
temporarily blocked from a clear view of it. That he
could carry off his speech naturally is irrelevant. The
point is that the arrangement of the playhouse ne-
cessitated the description. By the same token, when

6. I count 572 property identifications.
7. Distance alone would have justified the naming of properties as small as rings, keys, and handkerchiefs.

Richard says to the gentleman who defends Anne in *Richard III,* "Advance thy halberd higher than my breast" (I.ii.40), he is serving the dramaturgical function of informing spectators masked from the action that the First Gentleman is at that instant pointing his halberd at him. And in *Richard II* (I.i.69), Bolingbroke identifies the gage[8] he throws at the foot of Mowbray, partly because it would be masked from spectators facing either his own back or Mowbray's. So too, when Imogen moves upstage toward the cave (very likely the inner space) in *Cymbeline*[9] and specifically announces, twice within the scope of two lines (III.vi.25–26), that now she has her sword out, she does so partly for the benefit of spectators who face her back. Indeed, the drawing of swords is always accompanied in the plays by a specific announcement.[10]

What pertains to the clear perception of properties equally applies, of course, to the comprehension of stage business performed without them. Thus to guarantee that spectators on all three sides of his platform stage simultaneously will perceive the by-play between Hermione and Polixenes in *The Winter's Tale,* as well as to call attention to the reaction of the jealous husband, Shakespeare has Leontes describe the action,

8. In *Richard II* the gage, a glove that, when thrown at the feet of an opponent, signifies a challenge to combat, is named in the dialogue every time it is brought into use.

9. That Shakespeare continued to employ the convention in his last three romances, performed at Blackfriars, where the audience is presumed to have faced the front of the stage, is not surprising. Among the arguments for not dropping it is the generally accepted fact that the romances were written for the public Globe stage as well.

10. Even when two actors face each other with foils, as during the duel in *Hamlet,* spectators who stand or sit behind either player are certain to miss some of the action visually.

as it occurs, in detail.[11] Likewise, the bodies of actors would have obstructed the vision of widely scattered groups of spectators during a crowded scene like the blinding of Gloucester in *King Lear*, necessitating the successive descriptive comments which appear in the dialogue (III.vii.67–85). Equally essential is the descriptive line in *Macbeth* delivered as Lady Macbeth begins to wring her hands while sleepwalking. Despite his preceding question, "What is it she does now?"— which would have succeeded in drawing attention to the sleepwalker, if that had been the dramatist's sole purpose—the attending doctor is made to add the specific description, "Look how she rubs her hands" (V.i.30). Standing beside the gentlewoman to whom he addresses his remarks, the doctor is obliged to give an exact account because otherwise spectators behind the two, unable to see clearly the hand rubbing, would have lost much of the value of Lady Macbeth's ensuing monologue. For a similar purpose the dialogue in Shakespeare's plays consistently describes changes in the facial expressions of the actors[12] and invariably identifies weeping.[13]

Impressive as evidence also are requests for action at which recipients rebel or disobey outright.[14] It seems significant that whenever a character postpones compliance with such a direction, the dramatist notifies the audience of the delay by having the command repeated. In the few cases where an actor refuses completely to perform the direction, the dialogue tells of

11. I.ii.115–17, 125–26, and 183–85.
12. See, for example, *3 Henry VI*, III.ii.82; *The Comedy of Errors*, II.ii.112; and *Othello*, V.ii.38, 43.
13. See *2 Henry VI*, I.i.115; *Titus Andronicus*, III.i.136–37; and *Much Ado About Nothing*, IV.i.256–60.
14. See *1 Henry IV*, II.i.38–45; *As You Like It*, I.i.68–69; and *The Tempest*, II.ii.145–46, 158.

his refusal. Hence in *1 Henry VI* when Joan Pucel silently refuses to kneel at the request of the shepherd (V.iv.25), he immediately informs the audience of the fact by adding, "Wilt thou not stoop?" If either the shepherd or one of Joan's several captors in the scene masks her from the view of some spectators, his words are their only signal that she actually has not knelt.

An obstruction other than the backs of actors or the intervening bodies of others is evident in Iago's command to Roderigo, "Here, stand behind this bulk" (*Othello*, V.i.1). Iago is probably referring to a permanent fixture on the Globe stage, one of the two posts supporting the "heavens."[15] These posts, occasionally, at least, must have prevented some spectators from seeing bits of stage business clearly (especially those in the rear galleries viewing action on the inner space)—another strong reason for inserting descriptions into the dialogue.

The dramatist must have been thoroughly convinced of the usefulness of such a device before venturing to employ it so freely, for there would always have been present a majority of spectators who saw and heard what went on—spectators to whom a lack of synchronization between the action and the word or a discrepancy of any kind would have been, at best, distracting. Descriptions delivered along with the action[16] would have demanded perfect timing of the players; descriptions after the action[17] would have required that

15. In the Folio the quarto's "Bulke" becomes "Barke," possibly meaning a tree.

16. I count 607 instances. Especially difficult to time must have been cases where one actor has to describe the pantomiming of a second and third, as in Iago's long aside, which details the stage business between Cassio and Desdemona (*Othello*, II.i.168–78).

17. I count 1153.

it had been previously performed in exact accordance; and identification of a stage property would have made it difficult for an actor who had forgotten to bring it on the stage to cover his error by faking. Only the potential masking of important business or essential properties would have warranted thus limiting the freedom of the performer and endangering the success of the performance.

Whenever he could afford to do so, as a matter of fact, Shakespeare seems to have dispensed with specific description. Hence numerous references are worded too generally to permit the auditory perception of stage business. For example, though a second glance at the text may tell the reader that Lear is really striking his head when he shouts, "O Lear, Lear, Lear! / Beat at this gate that let thy folly in" (I.iv.292–93), such dialogue seems to be too unspecific to have helped an audience which so much of the time, as we have seen, had to depend for perception on the ears alone. The explanation for vague references like this in Shakespeare, however, is clearly given in a stage direction of *Coriolanus*. Having put four Volsces to flight, Caius Marcius remonstrates with his enthusiastic followers in words almost wholly undescriptive of their action:

> O, me alone? Make you a sword of me?
> If these shows be not outward, which of you
> But is four Volsces?

What the hero means by "Make you a sword of me?" and "these shows" is specifically detailed in the marginal notation of the Folio, which reads, *"They all shout and wave their swords, take him up in their arms and cast up their caps"* (I.vi.75). Since this action must have been visible above the bodies of the players, all the original spectators, regardless of position, should have been able not only to hear the soldiers shout, but also to see them wave their swords above their heads, lift Marcius on to their shoulders, and cast their caps into the air. Here the dramatist need not have Caius Marcius describe the action, since everyone in the audience can be expected to perceive it. Likewise anyone in the audience should have been able to see Lear lift his hand above his head to strike it. The general visibility of such stage business freed Shakespeare from the usual obligation of writing specific description into the accompanying dialogue.

That the dramatist resorted to the convention only when the comprehension of the Elizabethan audience required it seems further demonstrated by stage business noted in the margin of the basic text which is accompanied by no descriptive dialogue whatever, general or specific. Thus the dialogue does not mention the business referred to by two notations in *3 Henry VI: "Takes off his crown"* (IV.iii.48) and *"Lays his hand on his head"* (IV.vi.68).[18] The actions must have been visible, as that of Lear was, above the bodies of intervening players. Even more obviously visible to the entire house would have been the stage business described by the notation alone in the quarto of *Titus Andronicus, "They all kneel"* (I.i.388). Similarly, the notation *"Drinks,"* repeated in one scene of *The Tempest* (II.ii.47, 57), identifies a piece of business enacted by Stephano[19] in the presence of Trinculo and Caliban while they lie prone on the stage floor, where

18. The spelling of these two stage directions and of those that follow is modernized, but the words are those appearing in the basic texts.

19. In *1 Henry IV* (II.iv.132 and 172) two notations refer to Falstaff's taking a drink in the company of other characters who are standing. Possibly this scene was enacted in an inner space, where it would have been less likely that any other character could have blocked Falstaff from view.

they could hardly mask him from the general view. As evidently visible is the gesture, again not referred to in the dialogue, of the ghost in *Hamlet, "It spreads his arms"*[20] (I.i.127), for the perception of outspread arms could hardly have been blocked by the back of the ghost or by the body of any member of the watch onstage at the time. Nor does the final example, in *Cymbeline, "Imogen awakes"* (IV.ii.291), require allusion in the dialogue, for all that is necessary is to have her speak, which she does immediately, in horror at the gruesome spectacle of her headless companion. Moreover, no standing player is present to mask her from view. I detect no other notations without dialogue reference of any kind which can be accurately considered as concerning stage business, action a player performs without changing his position on the stage.

Of all stage movement, as distinct from stage business, the two types most frequently noted in the margin of the basic texts are, of course, entrances and exits. While doing either, a player is obviously shifting his position in relation to the sight lines of the audience. Thus if at one instant he is masked from a given group of spectators by the intervening body of another player, the next his walk will bring him past the obstruction and into their view. The same applies to shifts in position other than entrances or exits, eliminating the necessity for description in the dialogue of any kind of lateral movement. And as with stage business performed above the heads of players, the general visibility of vertical movement upward (not downward, as through trapdoors) would also have obviated the necessity of spoken description. Hence the well known

20. Kittredge emends this to read "Spreads his arms," and seems to assign it to Horatio rather than the ghost. His conjecture, however, does not affect my argument.

marginal notation in the Folio text of *Antony and Cleopatra,* "*They heave Antony aloft to Cleopatra*" (IV.xv.37), requires no spoken description because it concerns a shift of position, from one stage level to another, that is visible to the whole audience. All action noted in the margin without dialogue description is in the one category: it includes either stage business that everyone in the audience must have been able to see at the same time, or stage movement whose very nature makes it visible at one time or another to the entire house.[21]

Thus Shakespeare's periods of silence during stage action prove what his verbal descriptions demonstrate: he made every possible effort to ensure that every member of his public playhouse audience perceived the whole of every play—through the eyes whenever practicable; through the ears whenever there was danger of masking. And though the dramatist originally employed his directions in the dialogue for reasons far different from purposes of publication, how welcome they are today to the reader of his plays—the modern reader, whose visual perception is masked from all of Shakespeare's stage business by the passage of time.

21. It is possible that the stage itself, let alone the actors, was not visible to the entire house. But a playwright cannot be expected to do much for spectators who are unfortunate enough to sit behind posts or who are blocked for the duration of the performance from seeing the stage by the bulk, or large hats, of those in front.

THREE

Stage Business in the Margins of the Basic Texts

☞ From time to time during this century, theater directors, including those most experienced in producing Shakespeare, have expressed their puzzlement concerning both the paucity of italicized marginal directions in the pre-1623 quartos and the First Folio and their uselessness in catching the picture of the stage action as the dramatist originally had conceived of it. The unadorned statement "They fight. Tybalt falls" in *Romeo and Juliet,* for example, is of little help to members of a modern production either as to the time to be allotted to the duel or to the details of the stage business entailed. And a direction occurring frequently in the basic texts, "Alarums and Excursions," which may have originally served for an entire sequence of marchings and counter marchings, trumpets and drums, victories and defeats, leaves far too much to the imagination of the acting company faced with it.

Such has never been the practice of modern playwrights, some of whom, as everyone has noticed, interrupt the dialogue of their plays with marginal notations so copious that the reader is obliged sometimes to wade through a myriad of italicized descriptions of everything imaginable, including titles of books on the library shelves of the setting, before he can return to the normal interchange of speech between the characters in the drama.

Thus in sharp contrast to the nearly three thousand directions for stage business in the dialogue itself, discussed in the preceding chapter, I have managed to tabulate only 320 marginal[1] directions (exclusive of *Enter, Exit*) in the first authentic printings of the plays, none of which are helpful today. Such notations, not enlightening to the modern director, could hardly have been intended originally to instruct Shakespeare's fellows in the specific details of their stage business. What could have been their purpose?

A close analysis of all the notations seems to indicate at least one solution: a great many, though admittedly not all, seem to be primarily not so much directions to the players as warnings to the prompter to expect momentary interruptions in the normal flow of the dialogue. Three notations,[2] all appearing in the First Folio, actually denote silence in their wording: the best known instance describes business between the hero of *Coriolanus* and his mother:

> *Holds her by the hand silent.*   (V.iii.182)

The second, appearing in the early *1 Henry VI*, concerns the fiends conjured up by Joan Pucel:

> *They walke, and speake not.*   (V.iii.12)

And the third, in *3 Henry VI*, marks the entrance of Warwick and his followers for their attack on Edward, Duke of York, in his tent:

1. I use the term "marginal" for convenience rather than accuracy, to denote notations of stage business which are not part of the dialogue. Actually, many such notations are interlineated between speeches rather than printed in either side margin.

2. A fourth notation of the type *"Silence"* appears in the Folio text of *The Winter's Tale* at III.ii.10, though modern editors seem to feel that this word properly belongs in the dialogue.

> *Enter Warwicke, Clarence, Oxford, Somerset,*
> *and French Souldiers, silent all.*   (IV.iii.22)

Two other notations, appearing in both the first quarto and the Folio texts of *Titus Andronicus,* seemingly indicate silence of some duration on the stage:

> *He writes his name with his staffe, and*
> *guides it with feete and mouth.*
> (IV.i.68–69)

> *Shee takes the staffe in her mouth, and*
> *guides it with her stumps and writes.*
> (IV.i.76)

In the same play appears still a third direction which marks an interval of silence:

> *Andronicus lieth downe, and the Iudges*
> *passe by him.*   (III.i.11)

In the first good quarto of a later play, *Romeo and Juliet,* is found this notation, which also describes business (or movement) without dialogue:

> *They march about the Stage, and Seruingmen*
> *come forth with Napkins.*   (I.iv.114)

And noted in the first quarto of *1 Henry IV* is this piece of business, which is carried out by Falstaff and his cronies without verbal comment:

> *Here they rob them and bind them.*
> (II.ii.97)

Marked also in the earliest authentic texts are the dumb show in *Hamlet* (III.ii.145) and the several pantomimes in *Cymbeline* (V.iii.94, V.iv.29, 92) and *The Tempest* (III.iii.19, 52, 82, IV.i.138, V.i.57), all of which require varying intervals of silence on the stage during their performance. Since these last, however, are more fully descriptive than the usual marginal notation, they might readily have proved more helpful to the players than to the book-holder.

Such does not seem the case, on the other hand, with the brief notations which indicate the silent reading of letters. In *3 Henry VI* appears this one:

> *They all reade their Letters.* (III.iii.166)

Though "They" refers only to Warwick, Lewis, and Margaret—leaving Oxford and Edward to comment aloud on the facial reactions of the letter readers—the wording of the comments implies that they begin to talk only after a definite pause in the dialogue. Certainly the notation "Reads" in *Richard III* (I.iv.91), which refers to Brakenbury's silent reading of the commission for the fate of Clarence, allows for no accompanying dialogue, for it is Brakenbury himself who is the next to break the silence. Likewise, the notation of Saturninus' perusal of the letter he receives from the clown in *Titus Andronicus:*

> *He reades the Letter* (IV.iv.44)

requires an interval of silence, because Saturninus himself has the next line of dialogue. Twice in *Antony and Cleopatra* (I.iv.beginning and IV.i.beginning) Octavius enters reading a letter silently, and both times he himself is the first to speak aloud. And in *Cymbeline* (III.ii.beginning), the notation

> *Enter Pisanio reading of a Letter*

comes at a point where Pisanio is alone, with no one else around who could speak aloud while he studies silently the charges brought by Posthumus against Imogen.

Another interesting group of marginal notations which mark intervals of what must have been silence, at least as far as the prompter was concerned, are directions that indicate whispering between characters on the stage. In the early *1 Henry VI* (III.ii.59) is to be found

> *They whisper together in counsell.*

In *Richard III* appears this much briefer note:

> *Whispers.* (IV.ii.79)

In *King John* there is

> *Whispers with Blanch.* (II.i.503)

In *Julius Caesar:*

> *They whisper.* (II.i.100)

In a considerably later play, *Antony and Cleopatra,* there appears

> *Whispers in's Eare.* (II.vii.44)

And in the dramatist's last unaided work, *The Tempest,* is the direction

> *Iuno and Ceres whisper, and send Iris on*
> *employment.* (IV.i.124)

These are the only notations of their kind in the basic texts of Shakespeare's plays, and they all mark instances in which nothing but whispering is taking place at the time. For in those few cases where a character refers aloud to someone else's whispering,[3] no notation of the stage business appears in the text. It seems, then, that the prompter was informed by a notation in the book he held whenever whispering was to take place without accompanying dialogue—whenever the

---

3. See *3 Henry VI,* I.i.149; *King John,* II.i.475; and *Othello,* II.i.169.

only speech on stage was to be delivered in the almost if not altogether complete silence of the whisper.

But by no means is it to be understood that the marginal directions in Shakespeare are confined only to intervals of silence or even near silence. On the contrary, an imposing number of notations mark interruptions in the dialogue which would seem to be anything but quiet. Such, for example, would appear to be the numerous notations in the basic texts that denote pitched battles or skirmishes on stage. A series from *1 Henry VI* is typical:

> *Here they fight, and Ioane de Puzel ouer-
> comes.* (I.ii.103)
>
> *Here they skirmish againe.* (I.iii.69)
>
> *Here they fight.* (I.v.8)
>
> *They fight againe.* (I.v.12)

Doubtless the book-holder could hear the noise produced by such actions, but they are noted in the texts, I believe, chiefly because no dialogue accompanies them. It seems significant, at any rate, that every time a fight takes place without accompanying dialogue, the event is marked in the text.[4] Even when a victim gets no opportunity to strike back, so that the action is relatively brief, the attack is noted in the early texts. In *3 Henry VI*, for example, as each of the three Yorkist brothers takes a share in the murder of Prince Edward, his action is separately noted:

4. See *2 Henry VI*, II.iii.95, IV.iii.beginning, IV.vii.beginning, and IV.x.63; *3 Henry VI*, II.iv.11; *1 Henry VI*, I.v.32, III.i.91, 103; *Richard III*, V.v.beginning; *Romeo and Juliet*, I.i.70, III.i.136; *1 Henry IV*, II.ii.108, V.iii.13, V.iv.38, 43, 74, 76; *Othello*, II.iii.157; *King Lear*, V.iii.150; *Macbeth*, V.vii.11, V.viii.8, 34; *Coriolanus*, I.iv.29, 61, 62, I.viii.13, III.i.229; and *Cymbeline*, V.ii.beginning, 10, 13.

Stabs him.	(V.v.38)
Rich. stabs him.	(39)
Clar. stabs him.	(40)

And instances of similar notations are scattered throughout the texts of other plays.[5] Surely the various fights (if not stabbings) in Shakespeare must have differed from one another somewhat in detail. Yet not one of the marginal notations attempts to describe the peculiarities of the particular conflict. It would appear, then, that these notations, like those which seem to indicate intervals of silence, were not written, as has sometimes been assumed, for the benefit of the actors, but rather for the sake of the prompter.

Why should he be informed of an interruption in the normal flow of the dialogue? The answer, I believe, is so that he would not be tempted to prompt every time there was a cessation of dialogue. It doesn't take much experience as a director in the theater to realize that no one can prompt effectively unless he has attended a number of rehearsals and followed the text closely. He must learn to know each player's style, and to know whether he is pausing for effect or has forgotten his lines, for as every actor who has ever performed in any play knows, nothing is more irritating than to be prompted unnecessarily. Whether or not Shakespeare's prompter attended all rehearsals and thereby learned where pauses in the dialogue were intentional no one can tell. But it is known that

5. See *2 Henry VI*, I.iii.141, IV.vi.9; *1 Henry VI*, I.iv.69, III.iv.37; *Richard III*, I.iv.275 and IV.iv.507; *The Comedy of Errors*, II.ii.23, IV.iv.47; *Titus Andronicus*, II.iii.116, IV.ii.145, V.iii.63; *The Taming of the Shrew*, I.ii.17, II.i.22, 220, IV.iii.31; *Henry V*, IV.viii.9, V.i.30; *Othello*, V.ii.235; *King Lear*, III.vii.80; *Antony and Cleopatra*, II.v.61, 62; *Coriolanus*, IV.v.36, 54, V.vi.131.

Shakespeare's Playhouse Practice

Shakespeare's company played repertory and in the course of a week might perform as many as three to half a dozen different plays. Under such circumstances, a prompter could ill afford to trust to his memory the spots for pauses that were intentional. How much simpler to mark, perhaps during rehearsal, the places for such gaps in the dialogue as pantomimes, whispering, and fights not already noted by the dramatist himself. No wonder such notations prove almost valueless to the modern director, whose primary interest is in the details of the stage business rather than in the location of interruptions in the dialogue.

How, it might be asked, could Shakespeare's prompter have determined, after the beginning of an interruption, exactly when to resume active prompting of dialogue; how could he have known whether the action without dialogue still continued or whether it was finished and the next speaker had really forgotten his lines? In other words, how long a pause was necessary to cover a pantomime, a whisper, a fight? He could have afforded to put his finger on the marked place, to take his eyes from the book, and to look at the action if he was in a position to see it. If he was not (which, in the absence of "wings" on the main stage, is more likely), it seems reasonable to suppose that the prompter could sense the end of a lengthy interruption, like a scuffle, from the thud, say, made by the loser's falling body.[6] For the duration of a whisper or the silent reading of a letter, the prompter could allow the actor some leeway before giving the cue for the next line. Certainly a prompting slightly delayed

6. Interesting with regard to this conjecture is a notation to be found in both the good quarto and the Folio texts of *Romeo and Juliet* (III.i.136): "They Fight. Tibalt falles," mentioned on p. 23, above.

would inflict less damage on the performance than
one given out of place.

In this connection it may be interesting to note that
many of the marginal directions in Shakespeare mark
interruptions that must have been of short duration
indeed. Such are the pauses in the dialogue created by
kisses on stage,[7] though it should be added that not
all kisses in the plays are marked. Such, too, must have
been the business marked by the simple notation
"dies"[8] or "sleeps."[9] On the other hand, it is possible
that notations such as these were originally intended
as reminders to the players in rehearsal rather than as
warnings to the book-holder not to prompt during the
brief pause that ensued.

More likely intended for the benefit of the prompter are the numerous notations for reading documents
aloud on the stage.[10] Technically, to be sure, a player
who reads aloud is not interrupting the flow of the
dialogue. But whether the words were originally in
the playhouse book or not, almost everyone agrees
that they were written on the scroll which the actor

7. See *1 Henry VI,* V.iii.184; *Othello,* V.ii.15; *Antony and Cleopatra,* III.ii.65.

8. See *King John,* IV.iii.10; *Julius Caesar,* III.i.77, V.iii.90, V.v.51; *Othello,* V.ii.251, 359; *Antony and Cleopatra,* V.ii.316, 331.

9. See *Richard III,* V.iii.118; *A Midsummer Night's Dream,* III.ii.436; *Cymbeline,* II.ii.10.

10. See *2 Henry VI,* I.iv.61; *Titus Andronicus,* II.iii.267; *Love's Labour's Lost,* IV.i.60, IV.iii.59, 100; *Romeo and Juliet,* I.ii.66; *The Merchant of Venice,* II.ix.62; *1 Henry IV,* II.iii.beginning; *Much Ado About Nothing,* V.iii.2; *Julius Caesar,* II.i.45; *As You Like It,* IV.iii.39, 44; *Twelfth Night,* V.i.310; *Hamlet,* II.ii.115; *All's Well That Ends Well,* III.ii.20, III.iv.3, V.iii.138; *King Lear,* I.ii.47, IV.vi.266, V.iii.109; *Macbeth,* I.v. beginning; *Timon of Athens,* V.iv.69; *Cymbeline,* I.vi.21, III.iv.20, V.iv.137, V.v.434.

held in his hands, making prompting not only unnecessary but annoying. The player, then, could pause during his reading without fear of untimely interruption from the prompter.[11] Marginal notations for songs[12] in the texts would be more difficult to explain were it not that we know on the best authority that these also were written on scrolls. It is interesting to note, in this regard, the omission of lyrics after the notation "Catch sung" in the First Folio text of *Twelfth Night* (II.iii.75).

Only one other song in all Shakespeare, however, omits the words from the printed text: in both the Quarto and Folio of *1 Henry IV* appears the notation:

> *Here the Ladie sings a welsh song.*
>
> (III.i.247)

But both texts mark as well the three occasions on which Lady Mortimer speaks:

> *The Ladie speakes in Welsh.*   (III.i.199)

11. The words on the scroll, it goes without saying, might also have been written in the promptbook. The duplication would not only have safeguarded the company against the loss of the scroll but would also have indicated to the book-holder exactly where he was to resume prompting. It is perhaps interesting to note that in the only instance where the same words are read aloud twice, the prophecy of the lion's whelp in *Cymbeline* (V.iv.138–45 and V.v.435–42), both printings in the Folio are identical, even to spelling, punctuation, hyphenation, and spacing of the letters. Could this by any chance indicate that the prophecy did not appear in the playhouse manuscript but had to be printed from the one scroll both times?

12. See *A Midsummer Night's Dream*, II.ii.8; *The Merchant of Venice*, III.ii.62; *As You Like It*, II.v.39; *Twelfth Night*, II.iii.39, V.i.397; *Hamlet*, IV.v.22; *The Winter's Tale*, IV.iii.beginning; *The Tempest*, I.ii.374, 395, II.i.299, II.ii.43, 181, III.ii.129, IV.i.105, V.i.87.

> *The Ladie againe in welsh.*   (203)
>
> *The Ladie speakes againe in Welsh.*   (211)

In all four cases perhaps the prompter, unable to fathom Welsh, needed these warnings of foreign sounds coming from the stage so that he would not suspect that the actor in the part of Lady Mortimer had somehow been reduced to uttering mere gibberish!

Thus the evidence in the original texts of Shakespeare's plays seems to point to the conclusion that a great number of the so-called stage directions, so unhelpful to directors today, were originally intended only for the use of the book-holder, as warnings to be fully prepared for intentional interruptions in the normal flow of the dialogue, so that he would not be misled into thinking that the players had forgotten their lines.

FOUR

An Intermediate Stage Level for Fast Ascents and Descents

When Bernardo uses the words "upon the platform where we watch'd" (*Hamlet,* I.ii.213) to locate for Hamlet the appearance of the ghost in the preceding scene, is he really, it should be asked, referring simply to the permanent stage of the Globe Theatre, or rather to scaffolding superimposed upon the stage[1] for a discoverable purpose other than supporting the throne present in all plays with royal characters?[2] Hamlet himself repeats the term as he promises to visit Bernardo, Horatio, and Marcellus "upon the platform" in a later scene (I.ii.251–53). If both references are but to the bare stage, as has normally been accepted, it would seem a little strange that no other examples like them appear in all Shakespeare.[3]

1. Both C. T. Onions (*A Shakespeare Glossary,* 1931, p.163) and the *Oxford English Dictionary* (VII, 966)) give the meaning of *platform* as used in *Hamlet* as a "level place constructed for mounting guns in a fort."

2. At times royal personages are "discovered" seated on the throne when the inner-space curtain opens. Macbeth says to his supper guests, "Our hostess keeps her state," which indicates that Lady Macbeth remains in the spacious throne after her husband has descended to mingle with his guests.

3. The term "platform" in any sense occurs in only two other lines. In *1 Henry VI* (II.i.77) Joan uses the word figuratively, her "platforms" designating strategic plans against the English; and in *Othello* (II.iii.125) Montano refers to a location offstage.

Moreover, the opening scene of *Hamlet* has Bernardo, Horatio, and Marcellus each take a turn at requesting his fellows to sit down, a circumstance which has misled more than one theater director and commentator into the hesitant conclusion that furniture obtrusively inappropriate to the scene must have been placed on the stage for the occasion.

Anyone entertaining the notion would surely have agreed that a raised platform on the stage would have offered the watch more suitable seating space than unbecoming stools. At one point in the scene Bernardo says to the others, "Sit down awhile" (I.i.30), yet three lines later Horatio is given the reiteration, "Well, sit we down." Does it not appear likely that the interval between the two speeches was needed for the men to mount a raised platform?

Indeed only such a structure can explain the fact that some ascents and descents in other plays require no more than three lines of dialogue to accomplish. In the Folio text of *Richard II*, for example, appears the stage direction,

> . . . *Enter on the Walls, Richard, Carlile [sic]*
> *Aumerle, Scroop, Salisbury.*   (III.iii.61)

Are the "Walls" here what they normally appear to be in Shakespeare, the balcony stage of the public playhouse?[4] Two aspects of the situation indicate that Richard and his retinue very likely entered on to a piece of scaffolding superimposed on the lower platform stage. In the first place, the playwright gives the royal company only three lines to descend for a meeting with Bolingbroke on the main stage: Richard's final line

4. Since the term "walls" is used throughout the basic texts interchangeably, the only way to discover whether it refers to the balcony or to a structure superimposed on the main stage is to examine the situation where the word appears.

from the "walls" is immediately followed by Bolingbroke's one-line request of Northumberland—

> What says his Majesty?   (III.iii.184)

which is more likely only a half line[5]—and after Northumberland's less than two-line reply, he says to Bolingbroke, concerning Richard,

> . . . Yet he is come.

Richard could not possibly have made his descent
from the balcony stage to the lower main stage in less
time than it took to say three lines. In the first place,
experiments with a stop watch on the Folger Library
stage[6] have proved that a descent by one actor alone
would require from five to six lines of blank verse at
the very least, twice the time Shakespeare allots the
actor in the part of Richard. And in the second place,
neither Quarto nor Folio text contains a stage direction for either the exit (from the balcony stage) or the
re-entrance (on to the lower main stage) of Richard
and his followers—a most unusual omission if the balcony stage, as is usually supposed, was used in the
scene. If the original Richard descended merely from
a raised platform, on the other hand, the omission becomes completely understandable. And it goes without
saying that the player in the part could easily have
completed his descent within the time Shakespeare
has given him, particularly if his scaffolding had but
the four steps leading from it discovered many years
ago in a minor play of the period, *The Dumb Knight.*
For after the stage direction (III.i) *Enter Chip, Shav-
ing and a third with a scaffold,* Mariana's speech in

5. It is printed as such in modern editions.
6. The experiments were conducted years ago, and it is at
least doubtful that the distance to be traveled at the Folger is
exactly that at the old Globe.

ascending shows that the stairs brought on with the scaffold consisted of four steps:

> This first step lower
> Mounts to this next; this thus and thus hath
> brought
> My body's frame unto its highest throne.[7]

It may be more than coincidental that the number of lines given to Mariana for her ascent up these four steps matches exactly the number allotted to Richard II for his descent.

In two plays it seems the playwright considered a single line of dialogue sufficient to cover a descent. However, the first instance, in the early drama *1 Henry VI* (V.iii.144), very possibly concerns the balcony stage, for Regnier has not only the line spoken by Suffolk—

> And here I will expect thy coming

but also the stage notation "Trumpets sound," to cover his movement from one stage level to another. Besides, the Folio text marks the completion of Regnier's descent with *Enter Reignier,* possibly a superfluous direction for an actor who merely descends a scaffold in full sight of the audience. But the case in *King Lear* (II.i.21) is not so clear. At the end of a five-line soliloquy given after the exit of Curan, Edmund suddenly says,

> . . . Brother, a word! Descend! Brother, I
> say! . . .

and then immediately begins an intimate conversation with his brother, Edgar. Where could Edgar have been when his brother commanded him to descend? The

7. The term "throne" is very likely not accidental.

An Intermediate Stage Level

Folio prints *Enter Edgar* immediately above Edmund's command for the descent.[8] Does this stage direction refer to a re-entrance on to the main stage after a descent from the balcony stage? Hardly, for the only preceding stage direction, the one which opens the scene, reads, *Enter Bastard* [Edmund], *and Curan severally,* there being no notation for a previous entrance of Edgar's. Moreover, if Edgar had appeared on the balcony for any length of time before Edmund's command to descend, he would doubtless have overheard enough to become aware of his bastard brother's plot against him. And it is possible that *Enter Edgar* may have been added to the Folio version for the sake of the reader. But the main point is that Edgar could not feasibly have disappeared from the balcony stage, re-entered on to the main stage, and come close enough to Edmund for their intimate conversation in the brief time Shakespeare allots for his movement. The descent, then, must have been accomplished from a place on the stage considerably nearer to Edmund than the balcony stage.[9] And moving the notation *Enter Edgar* down three lines from its position in the Folio is not a satisfactory solution, though it has been offered as such, for if Edgar is to enter even that little later, then Edmund's lines

8. The "Pied Bull" quarto of 1608, generally regarded as an unauthentic text, prints the single word "Edgar" in the left-hand margin two prose lines before Edmund's request to descend.

9. It has been conjectured that Edgar descended from the third level of the tiring-house to the balcony, where Edmund is supposed to have stood. But we are informed by the text that Edmund could not have been in the balcony stage because the term "severally" in the entrance notation at the beginning of the scene refers to entrances through both main passageways on to the outer platform stage. The direction in the 1608 quarto reads, *Enter Bast.* [Edmund] *and Curan meeting.*

> . . . My father watches. O sir, fly this place!
> Intelligence is given where you are hid
> (II.i.22–23)

would have to be delivered to the empty air around
him while Edgar, to whom the advice is directed, hurries down the back stairway connecting the balcony
stage with the first level, out of earshot and out of
sight of both the audience and Edmund.

Pandarus and his niece in *Troilus and Cressida*
surely do not ascend to the balcony stage, because
their dialogue is continuous (I.ii.192–98) as they
shift from a lower level to an upper.[10] Pandarus and
Cressida are the only characters on the stage as the
Trojan heroes, including Troilus, are about to parade
in view one by one across the main stage. The dialogue
runs—

> *Pandarus.* Hark! they are coming from the
>   field. Shall we stand up here and see them
>   as they pass toward Ilium? Good Niece, do,
>   sweet niece Cressida!
> *Cressida.* At your pleasure.
> *Pandarus.* Here, here, here's an excellent
>   place; here we may see most bravely . . .

The obvious question, asked by earlier commentators,
is, what does Pandarus mean by the words "stand up
here"?

What, in this respect, could have represented the
"pulpit" from which both Brutus and Antony delivered their orations in *Julius Caesar*? Editions that

---

10. I am assuming that players had to disappear momentar-
ily from view to travel from the main stage to the balcony
stage or vice versa, that the stairs between the two levels were
hidden from the view of the audience. I have never encountered
any theories to the contrary.

bother to footnote the situation invariably state that it must have been the upper or balcony stage. Yet the stage direction in the Folio which opens the scene—

Enter Brutus and goes into the Pulpit

does not appear to indicate that Brutus entered on the upper stage, nor that he entered on the lower and then climbed the hidden stairway to the upper (he would have had to exit immediately to do so). As he is about to leave the scene after his oration, moreover, Brutus delivers the line

Good countrymen, let me depart alone, . . .
(III.ii.61)

—hardly an appropriate request from a character on the upper stage to others standing on the lower stage below. But even a more decisive refutation of the general opinion that the "pulpit" must have been the balcony stage is the revealing statement made by the third plebeian later in the scene, preceding the ascent of Antony into the same pulpit,

Let him go up into the public chair. . . .
(III.ii.69)

Certainly an Elizabethan actor would never call the balcony stage "the public chair." Thus it would appear more reasonable to deduce that Antony gave his oration, as Brutus had done before him, from the "state," so commonly used as a throne on the public stage. As has long been known the *state* was a very large chair that could accommodate two or three people and which was placed on a dais and overhung by a canopy. The term, of course, is but an abbreviation of the more formal phrase "chair of estate," which, incidentally, is one reason why the royal throne is sometimes referred to as "the chair." Furthermore, there is every reason to believe that the chair was removable from the dais and some evidence to conjecture that the whole assembly was set on rollers for easy shifting. So it would appear that if Caesar himself had conducted the senate session in the previous scene (III.i) from the throne of the state, a setting appropriate to the occasion of his crowning, the throne could readily have been transformed into a "pulpit" with the removal of the chair.[11] And if there is anything to the argument that the state normally occupied the inner space, the transformation could have been achieved smoothly enough behind the closed traverse curtain.[12] Since Brutus ascends to deliver his funeral oration from the very spot where Caesar had been stabbed and Antony succeeds Brutus on the royal dais, the staging takes on symbolic significance.

Only one minor objection hinders consideration of the "hill" in V.iii of *Julius Caesar* as the dais of the state with the throne removed, namely the direction *Enter Pindarus* in the Folio (added for the reader?) marking the end of the descent of Pindarus from the hill on which he had erroneously reported to Cassius the fate of Titinius. An entrance direction at the end of a descent is usually taken to mean that the actor

11. Considering the lively imagination of an Elizabethan audience, the state with the throne still standing on it could readily have been used as the pulpit—it is called "the public chair"—with Brutus and later Antony standing in front of or beside the significantly vacated throne. I should stage it so.

12. Such an argument must presuppose, of course, that after Caesar was stabbed in the neck by Casca, he haltingly descended from his "state" and ran the gauntlet of conspirators' swords down to the outer stage, where he finally fell at the feet of Brutus. That Shakespeare so carefully provides for the removal of Caesar's body at the end of the scene, by having Antony recall Octavius' servant to help him carry it, seems to warrant the assumption.

must have disappeared from sight (on the back stairway connecting the balcony stage with the main stage) while shifting his position from one level to the other. Yet if the "hill" in *Julius Caesar* is the balcony stage, as has sometimes been asserted, there would seem to be something queer about the line spoken by Cassius,

> This hill is far enough . . . ,   (V.iii.12)

coupled with the later request of Brutus,

> Come, poor remains of friends, rest on this rock.   (V.v.1)

Granted that pieces of stage property disguised as rocks are mentioned in Henslowe's Diary and were therefore probably used in productions of the rival Admiral's Company, it is almost impossible to imagine a master craftsman like Shakespeare causing his company to resort to the crude business of carrying big "rocks" or pushing "hills" on to the main stage in view of the audience when it would have been so much easier to make use of a familiar fixture like the dais of the state, or one of the steps leading up to it, for the episode in *Julius Caesar*. More to the point, if the "hill" is assumed to be the balcony stage, as the footnotes of editors tend to indicate, how difficult it becomes to justify the answer Titinius gives to Messala's query as to where the former left Cassius

> . . . With Pindarus his bondman, on this hill
> (V.iii.56)

when it is evident that Titinius himself, along with Messala, must have entered the main stage below. It is impossible to believe that Titinius, seeking out a man whose whereabouts he knew, makes the error of coming in on the wrong stage level and, further, that he finds Cassius on a stage level different from the one on

which he left him. Surely it is more sensible to con-
clude that by the phrase "on this hill" Titinius meant
some kind of structure on the main stage, especially
since "hill" in reference to some location on the stage
is very rare in Shakespeare.[13]

Moreover, if the dais of the state or some other
piece of scaffolding was employed regularly on Shakespeare's stage, the enigma of Cleopatra's monument
is comparatively easy to solve. In the Folio text of
Antony and Cleopatra (IV.xv.37) the eye-catching
direction

> *They heave Antony aloft to Cleopatra*

has proved to be so troublesome largely because the
usual assumption has been that Cleopatra and her
maids in waiting stood on the balcony stage for this
scene. In a production nearly fifty years ago, Antony
was actually dragged up through a balcony trap door
by crane and windlass! But since that time no commentator that I know of has offered a better solution,
which is really not surprising as long as Cleopatra's
monument continues to be pictured as the balcony
stage in the original production, which can be shown
to be an impossibility. For one thing, Richard Burbage, in the part of Antony, was a big man whose
weight was not a trifling matter. In this scene he is obviously helpless and therefore can offer no aid to those
who are struggling to raise him some fifteen feet above
the main stage. Clearly the term *heave* in the Folio direction means something other than tossing the dying
Antony high enough in the air and accurately enough
so that his body would neatly hurtle the balustrade at

13. The only other instance is in *3 Henry VI* (II.v.23), where
Henry, in soliloquy, says, "To sit upon a hill, as I do now," and
from the action that follows it is evident that he, too, refers to
some location on the lower stage rather than up in the balcony.

the front of the balcony and land, without disaster, at the feet of Cleopatra. And just as evidently the boy actors in the parts of Cleopatra, Charmian, and Iras—regardless of their collective muscle—would hardly have arms long enough to reach down to grasp Antony from the lifted hands of those below. And even if the miracle could somehow be brought off, Burbage would surely not be happy about playing his dying scene, which is moving, behind the bars of the railing of the balcony stage. Anyone acquainted with the Globe Theatre stage must agree that something more accessible than the balcony stage must have been available in the original performances. And what could have been more accessible than the dais, with the throne (upon which both Octavius and Cleopatra probably sat in turn during previous scenes) removed? Indeed without such a piece of scaffolding to receive the mortally wounded Antony, modern producers might be obliged to adopt an expedient as clumsy as that used by the Benson company in 1898, which entailed strips of linen being lowered, which the guards wound round Antony, and raising him on the butt-ends of their halberds, no less, helped the actresses above to hoist him over the balcony rail. How much simpler and how infinitely more effective was the version produced by Katherine Cornell a half century later, which employed a scaffold about five feet high for the heaving of Antony aloft.[14] The Cornell company required no

14. The production I saw took place in Boston. True, the dimming of the spotlights helped to carry the business off smoothly, but the lifting of the dying Antony to a platform lower than the heads of the guards could have been accomplished as cleanly on the Elizabethan sunlit stage. In the Boston production the scaffold was quietly set in place on the stage behind the closed front curtain while a brief scene was performed in front of the proscenium arch.

strips of linen, nor crane and windlass, to accomplish the feat with smoothness and dignity.

That the balcony stage of the public playhouse came into frequent use during the original performances of Shakespeare's plays there is little doubt. Certainly it was employed in the orchard scenes of *Romeo and Juliet* and very likely is indicated most of the time when "walls" are referred to in notations, especially of the history plays. In *Cymbeline* it is difficult to imagine Jupiter descending through anything else but the trap door of the balcony stage.

But there is equally strong evidence that instead of using the balcony stage for all ascents and descents, as has frequently been supposed, some must have depended upon a platform superimposed on the main stage.[15] Whether the platform was actually, as I believe, the dais of the state with throne removed or a scaffold brought on stage for the purpose is, of course, conjectural, as is the question of whether it was "discovered" (uncovered by the opening of the curtain) on the inner space or thrust on to the main stage—or, for that matter, fixed on the main stage (or inner space) throughout the action of the play. The

15. In addition to the examples given above there are the cases of Berowne and Hermione. In *Love's Labour's Lost* (IV.iii.79) Berowne's remark, "here sit I in the sky," could refer to a piece of scaffolding on the main stage rather than, as has been conjectured, to the balcony stage with a sturdy tree propped against it. And surely the "statue" of Hermione, which Paulina twice commands to "descend" (*The Winter's Tale*, V.iii.88, 99), must have stood on such a structure rather than in the balcony, because the effectiveness of the scene demands that Hermione come to life and descend in full view of the startled characters on the stage as well as the members of the theater audience.

point remains that Shakespeare utilized such a piece of scaffolding for ascents and descents that had to be enacted quickly and for otherwise impossible or ridiculously cumbersome tasks like the heaving of Antony aloft to Cleopatra.

FIVE

Artful Brevity in the Monologues

☞ Nearly every reader of Shakespeare soon becomes aware that the dramatist periodically halts the normal interchange of dialogue in his plays to insert one of the four types of monologue: soliloquy, apostrophe,[1] aside,[2] or scroll reading. It might be useful to investigate the stagecraft behind the number of lines expended on these conventions, thereby to determine what principles of playhouse practice seem to have influenced the limitations of length the playwright placed upon each kind of monologue.

A close study of all Shakespearean soliloquies seems at first to reveal but little, for they range in length from as many as seventy-two lines[3] down to only half a line,[4] or, as in one instance, even two words.[5] A few soliloquists in the earliest plays do show a tendency to be longer-winded[6] than their successors of later date, but there appears to be no sharp contrast according to period. In fact, most of the early plays with

1. Even the apostrophe delivered by a player alone on stage differs from the pure soliloquy in that it is neither a direct address to the audience nor "introspective." See Chapter VI, below.

2. The aside exchanged between actors is technically a form of dialogue rather than a monologue.

3. *3 Henry VI*, III.ii.124–95.

4. *Troilus and Cressida*, V.iii.95.

5. *Love's Labour's Lost*, IV.iii.22: "Ay me!" Cf. *Romeo and Juliet*, II.ii.25.

6. See *3 Henry VI*, II.v.1–54; *2 Henry VI*, I.i.214–59; *The Two Gentlemen of Verona*, II.vi.1–43; and *Richard II*, V.v.1–66.

exceptionally long soliloquies also contain examples of very brief ones.[7] The same Proteus who encompasses a whole scene with one soliloquy,[8] for instance, is limited to but three lines in another.[9]

Purposeful contrast in length seems to become evident, however, when we separate those soliloquies given by an actor while he is alone on the stage from those delivered while other actors lurk somewhere in the background as eavesdroppers. Soliloquies given in the presence of other actors are consistently shorter. Whenever this type of soliloquy threatens to exceed a reasonable maximum, moreover, the dramatist breaks it up into smaller sections with comments from the eavesdroppers. The longest overheard soliloquy, for example, is the one of thirty-eight lines spoken by Henry VI while two keepers listen from their hiding place. Comments from the keepers break this up into three pieces, the longest of which extends to only twenty-seven lines.[10] And a more drastic process of interruption is put upon Parolles' overheard soliloquy in *All's Well That Ends Well,* where the lords and soldiers in ambush divide what would have otherwise been a continuous monologue of thirty-two lines into fully nine separate sections.[11] But, as we should expect, a keen sense of good theater lies behind Shakespeare's practice of cutting his overheard soliloquies shorter than the others. For one thing, a long soliloquy unbroken by comments from the other players lurking in the background would run the danger of

7. For example: *3 Henry VI,* II.iii.1–5; *2 Henry VI,* I.ii.61–67; and *The Two Gentlemen of Verona,* IV.iii.1–3. *Richard II* contains only the one soliloquy.

8. See above, note 6.

9. *The Two Gentlemen of Verona,* I.i.159–61.

10. *3 Henry VI:* III.i.13–21, 24–25, 28–54.

11. IV.i.27–34, 37–47, 50–52, 54–55, 57–58, 60–61, 63, 66–67, 69.

Artful Brevity in the Monologues

letting the audience forget their existence in the stage picture. Also, these hidden actors are always there for a dramatic purpose: to listen to what the soliloquist is revealing. Their periodical comments serve to inform the audience that they are doing so.

In general, the dramatist's apostrophes are notably shorter than his soliloquies, a good number of them not extending beyond two lines. The longest is given by Timon[12] as he stands alone[13] on the stage and raves to all the gods against mankind. But being completely alone, Timon, of course, is in a position similar to that of the pure soliloquist who gives his monologue on a stage otherwise unoccupied: with no other players around who could possibly break into the delivery, the audience does not anticipate interruption. In contrast to this type, apostrophes delivered with other characters on stage are much briefer, one containing but three words.[14] Moreover, the very nature of all apostrophes tends to limit the number of lines that artistically can be allotted to their delivery. All are directly addressed to abstractions,[15] inanimate objects,[16] or characters supposed to be incapable of hearing the words either because they are not on stage[17] the while

12. *Timon of Athens*, IV.i.1–41.

13. For differentiation between the kind of apostrophe given by Timon and the pure soliloquy, see note 1, above.

14. *The Taming of the Shrew*, I.ii.229.

15. For example: to "outrage" (*Richard III*, II.iv.63–65), to "Fortune" (*Romeo and Juliet*, III.v.60–65), to "Wit" (*Twelfth Night*, I.v.35–40), to "fate" (*Troilus and Cressida*, V.vi.25–26). I put in the same category the several apostrophes in the plays addressed to the "gods."

16. For example: to a sword (*2 Henry VI*, IV.x.72–76), to Pomfret Castle (*Richard III*, III.iii.8–13), to a picture of a "blinking idiot" (*The Merchant of Venice*, II.ix.56–57), to a vial of poison (*Romeo and Juliet*, V.i.85–86).

17. See *Richard III*, III.iv.91–92; *Much Ado About Nothing*, V.i.259–60; *Cymbeline*, IV.i.17–21; *The Winter's Tale*, II.ii.2–4.

or because they are corpses.[18] Such indirectness, ignoring both the living characters on stage and the audience at the same time, cannot be prolonged with much hope of success beyond closely defined limits. Thus it is not surprising to discover that the great majority of apostrophes in Shakespeare do not extend beyond ten lines, especially since most apostrophes,[19] unlike soliloquies, are delivered in front of characters obviously intended to hear them, who thereby would be expected by the audience to interrupt monologues of much greater length.

The aside in Shakespeare is usually shorter than either the soliloquy or apostrophe, the great majority being limited to from one to four lines. The total number of lines in a series of asides exchanged between two players, to be sure, may readily exceed the normal length of the single aside. Such a series (the most prolonged example in the plays) occurs in *Othello:* while the Moor writhes in the background out of earshot, Iago and Cassio carry on a dialogue about Bianca which extends to fully seventy-four lines.[20] And in *Measure for Measure*, Claudio and Lucio seem to interchange another long series.[21] But even series of asides between actors rarely continue unbroken for as long as these two. Asides to the audiences, being single speeches rather than exchanges, are notably briefer. By far the most garrulous deliverer of this type is Leontes, who ignores both Camillo and Mamillius on the stage with him for twenty-eight lines while he confides

18. See *2 Henry VI,* IV.x.86–90; *3 Henry VI,* II.ii.54–55; *1 Henry IV,* V.iii.22–24; *Julius Caesar,* V.iii.80–87; *Hamlet,* V.i.266–69.

19. More than half of the 216 apostrophes I detect in the plays.

20. IV.i.104–77.

21. I.ii.146–98, not marked as asides in Kittredge.

his growing jealousy to the audience.[22] No other character in the plays is permitted to prolong such an aside for even half so many lines.[23] The reason Shakespeare generally cut his asides shorter than soliloquies or apostrophes becomes evident when we consider the situation of the actor during delivery. While an aside is being given, at least one actor on the open stage with the speaker must be totally ignored. Until the aside is finished there are but two courses such an actor, who is not supposed to hear the words, can take: he can pretend to be occupied with something or someone else, or he can "freeze" (hold his position without movement and his facial expression without change). Now a player can become only so active about some other matter without running the risk of distracting the attention of the audience from the deliverer of the aside. And he can remain frozen in the picture for just so long without looking foolish. Hence the shorter the aside (especially when directed to the audience), the better for those actors on stage who must be ignored during the delivery.

When the actor playing the part of Celia in *As You Like It* entered the stage and read from a scroll[24] the thirty lines of Orlando's verses (III.ii.133-62) to Rosalind and Touchstone, he reached the top limit of time Shakespeare allows anyone to read aloud continuously.[25] And upon the reading of Orlando's poem the

22. *The Winter's Tale,* I.ii.180-207, sometimes considered as a soliloquy. But the text shows that the speaker is fully aware of the presence of the other characters; also, no character eavesdrops, which would not be the case with a soliloquy.

23. Second to Leontes is Macbeth, who ignores Ross, Angus, and Banquo for thirteen lines (*Macbeth,* I.iii.130-42).

24. Some scholars feel that such lines were written on the scrolls which the actors carried on stage.

25. Dumain's "sonnet," of twenty lines (*Love's Labour's Lost,* IV.iii.101-20), is the second longest continuous reading.

dramatist has Rosalind make the rather fitting comment:

> O most gentle pulpiter! what tedious homily
> of love have you wearied your parishioners
> withal and never cried, "Have patience, good
> people"!   (163–66)

Shakespeare, as with overheard soliloquies and asides to the audience, usually breaks scroll readings of any length into smaller sections, with comments from other characters on the stage at the time, or with observations from the reader himself. For illustration, Malvolio must read aloud (and we are glad he does) the entire twenty-eight lines of the letter planted for him by Maria—but Sir Toby, Fabian, and Malvolio himself break the delivery into four sections.[26] At another point in *Twelfth Night,* comments from Fabian divide Sir Toby's reading of the eighteen-line challenge written by Sir Andrew into six small parts.[27] But the thinnest slicing of a scroll reading is done in *The Two Gentlemen of Verona,* by Launce to Speed's rendition of the "catalog" which sets forth the virtues of Launce's milkmaid. Here the severed parts of a scroll of only twenty-three lines are spread over fully seventy-five lines of text.[28] Other scrolls that would otherwise lengthen out beyond a reasonable period of continuous reading time are treated less drastically but similarly. That scroll readings are cut so short is also dramaturgically sound practice. They are the most lifeless of all the conventions which depart from the normal play of dialogue. Whether a player actually

26. *Twelfth Night:* II.v.100–01, 107–10, 115–18, and 155–72.

27. III.iv.161–62, 164–66, 170–78, 176–77, 179–80, and 183–87.

28. III.i.302–76.

Artful Brevity in the Monologues

reads lines that are written on the scroll before him or merely holds a blank sheet and fakes the reading, the effect is the same. To show that he is reading rather than commenting on the contents of the scroll, his voice must take on a mechanical tone. His eyes must be on the scroll at least part of the time during delivery. The convention, in brief, forces the player to drop temporarily the intimate contact necessary to the lively interplay of emotions in the theater. For the time being, too, other actors on stage are pushed at least halfway out of the picture. What is worse, the audience feels it is being half shunned until the actor pockets his letter (or other type of scroll) and becomes a vital force again. The modern camera saves moving-picture audiences from this feeling by literally allowing them to read letters over the film player's shoulder. But even when, as over the radio, modern audiences cannot see the reader, the indirectness that must often creep into his voice when he reads becomes irritating if it continues too long. Thus when we examine the stagecraft of a playwright so conscious of the needs of his audience as William Shakespeare, we expect him not to prolong his readings of scrolls beyond the normal endurance of his customers. And, as with the other types of monologue, he lives up to expectations.

SIX

The Apostrophe

Though observations on the dramatist's employment of the soliloquy and aside abound,
there has hardly been any discussion[1] of what might
be considered a third classification of Shakespearean
monologue, the apostrophe. Yet there are actually
more than 200 apostrophes in Shakespeare, at least
one appearing in every play but two.[2] What seems to
be general hesitation about treating a device so frequently used in the plays may come, in part, from
some confusion about what an apostrophe really is.
The soliloquy and aside, possibly because they depend
largely on the stage picture at the time of delivery,
seem somewhat easier to detect. The soliloquy, of
course, requires that the actor giving it be alone on
stage or suppose that he is alone because the other actors present are hidden from his view.[3] The aside, if
delivered to the audience, demands at least one other
player on stage, obviously within earshot, who does
not hear it; if given to another actor, the aside requires
at least a third actor nearby who does not hear it. Considerable discussion has centered on whether particular

1. The only place I could discover in which the Shakespearean apostrophe is afforded even the briefest attention is
in a Columbia University doctoral dissertation dated 1911.

2. *The Comedy of Errors* and *The Merry Wives of Windsor.*

3. Of the 408 soliloquies I count in Shakespeare, fully 354
are delivered by a player who is completely alone on the stage
at the time.

Shakespearean soliloquies were originally delivered "introspectively" or in direct address to the audience. The aside is given normally in direct address either to the audience or to another player.[4] But under what circumstances can the apostrophe be delivered? What types of apostrophe are to be found in Shakespeare's plays?

In Shakespeare an actor can deliver an apostrophe either with or without other actors on stage. In either circumstance, however, he addresses his lines directly neither to other players on the stage with him nor to his audience. The only certain way to distinguish a Shakespearean apostrophe from either the ordinary soliloquy or the aside is through its wording. There is no problem of direct address to either the audience or another player, for all apostrophes are addressed to inanimate objects, to the gods, or to persons supposed to be incapable of hearing them at the time.

For example, there are numerous apostrophes to abstractions, like the one given by Portia to "love," while with bated breath she watches Bassanio about to choose one of the three caskets in *The Merchant of Venice:*

> . . . O love, be moderate; allay thy ecstasy;
> In measure rain thy joy; scant this excess!
> I feel too much thy blessing. Make it less
> For fear I surfeit!   (III.ii.111–14)

The actor playing the part of Portia could hardly have delivered this speech as direct address either to his audience or to Nerissa and Bassanio on stage with him. In the plays also are many apostrophes addressed to the gods, as in *Cymbeline* (III.vi.87–89), where

4. Some 300 asides are delivered directly to the audience and about 400 are exchanged between actors.

The Apostrophe

Imogen apostrophizes while Belarius and her incognito brothers whisper apart:

> . . . Pardon me, gods!
> I'ld change my sex to be companion with
> them,
> Since Leonatus' false.

This, assuredly, is meant to be not a confidence given directly to the audience, but a matter strictly between Imogen and the gods above her. Indeed, it is interesting to speculate whether actors giving this kind of apostrophe may not have looked in the direction of the actual playhouse "heavens" during the delivery.

Another large group of apostrophes addresses characters of the play who at the time are off the stage entirely. Such, for instance, is the apostrophe delivered by the Countess in *All's Well That Ends Well* to the absent Bertram, immediately after she reads in his letter that he has flown the French King's court:

> *Countess* (alone). This is not well, rash and un-
> bridled boy,
> To fly the favours of so good a king,
> To pluck his indignation on thy head
> By the misprizing of a maid too virtuous
> For the contempt of empire.
>   (III.ii.30–34)

Here the actor could readily have directed the whole speech to the letter he held in his hands. An interesting variety of apostrophe addressed to characters off the stage is that directed to an actor who is in the process of making his exit. In *Richard II* the gardener directs one such at the Queen immediately after her exit:

> Poor Queen, so that thy state might be no
> worse,

> I would my skill were subject to thy
>   curse! . . .   (III.iv.102–03)

Where originally the player faced to deliver this kind of apostrophe might seem to be a problem indeed, but there is little reason to suppose that he could not have faced squarely his audience in front of him. Almost everyone has seen this sort of thing happen in real life. An example which long ago came under my own notice occurred while I was a customer in a restaurant: the actors, a rather heavy-handed employer and an innocent but irate waitress. The dialogue ran as follows:

> *Employer* (to waitress). Why do you have to loaf so much of the time? Get to work!
> *Exit* (from the vicinity)
> *Waitress* (facing toward me). I could work a whole lot better if you'd stay out of the way.

Though her words were directed to her employer, she was careful to soften her delivery enough to keep it well out of his earshot. The whole affair was entirely natural, and the stage business in Shakespeare's playhouse may well have been based on such familiar incidents.

Some apostrophes in Shakespeare, on the other hand, are given to actors who are actually on the stage. In every case the object of the address is assumed to be incapable of hearing the words, either because he is "dead," like Hotspur when he receives the apostrophe from Prince Hal in *1 Henry IV,* beginning:

> . . . Fare thee well, great heart!
> Ill-weav'd ambition, how much art thou
>   shrunk! . . .[5]

5. The whole apostrophe to Hotspur appears at V.iv.87–101.

or because he simulates death, like Falstaff, who, while playing possum, gets an apostrophe[6] from Hal, beginning:

> . . . What, old acquaintance? Could not all
> this flesh
> Keep in a little life? Poor Jack, farewell! . . .[7]

or because he is "asleep," like both Richard and Richmond, who doze in their respective tents in *Richard III* while eleven successive apostrophes are addressed to each of them in turn by the ghosts of Richard's victims.[8]

Many apostrophes in Shakespeare do not confine themselves to one particular addressee. In *Cymbeline,* for instance, Posthumus consumes an entire scene[9] with a speech which directs his repentance impartially toward a bloody handkerchief, "you married ones,"[10] Pisanio (who is off the stage at the time), the gods, Britain, Imogen (also off the stage), and the gods again. This apostrophe, to be sure, must be considered also a soliloquy, for during its delivery the actor stands alone on the stage.[11] But since such speeches can hardly be

6. Even in this instance, as we might expect, the apostrophizer believes that his addressee is incapable of hearing his words.

7. The whole apostrophe, a continuation of the one delivered to Hotspur, appears at V.iv.102–10.

8. V.iii.119–77.

9. V.i.1–33.

10. It may be suspected that this phrase is a soliloquy and that "you married ones" could have been addressed directly to his audience. I prefer to think of it as an apostrophe addressed to everyone who happens to be married, whether present in the audience at the time or not.

11. In general, Shakespeare's apostrophes are much shorter than his soliloquies, which is understandable considering that most apostrophes occur in the presence of other players who are capable of interrupting. The longest apostrophe, given by

classified accurately as pure soliloquies and since numerous apostrophes in the plays are delivered by actors alone on the stage,[12] it would seem that for monologues of this type a new label should be coined—say, "apostrophe-soliloquy," or "soliloquy-apostrophe."

The great majority of apostrophes delivered with other actors on stage, as would be expected, are evidently overheard by them. Indeed, most apostrophes of this kind are so written as to include the others on stage in their very wording. For example, when Richard II apostrophizes in this manner to the absent Bolingbroke:

> . . . Proud Bolingbroke, I come
> To change blows with thee . . .
>
> (III.ii.188–89)

it is evident that he is spokesman also for Carlisle, Aumerle, Salisbury, Scroop, and the others on stage with him. *Cymbeline* offers an instance, indeed, where the other players on stage join the apostrophizer in a kind of refrain:

> *Belarius.* . . . Hail, thou fair heaven!
> We house i'th'rock, yet use thee not so
> hardly
> As prouder livers do.
> *Guiderius.* Hail, heaven!
> *Arviragus.* Hail, heaven! (III.iii.7–9)

On the other hand, a small but significant minority

Timon (*Timon of Athens,* IV.i, entire scene), extends to forty-one lines. The shortest, spoken by Lucentio (*The Taming of the Shrew,* I.ii.229), is of only three words. The normal length of the Shakespearean apostrophe, however, is from two to ten lines.

12. Some eighty-seven of the 216 apostrophes in Shakespeare's plays.

The Apostrophe

of Shakespearean apostrophes evidently go unheard by other actors on the stage who at the time are perfectly capable of hearing them.[13] These differ sharply from soliloquies, which are practically always overheard when other players are anywhere on the stage.[14] And though similar to asides in requiring other actors to be within earshot when delivered, the "unheard" apostrophe differs from the aside in that it is never addressed directly to the audience or to other actors. Of course, the only way the reader can pick out unheard apostrophes is to relate their content to the situation taking place in the play at the moment of their delivery. For example, in *Antony and Cleopatra* when Enobarbus addresses Antony, who is off the stage—

> . . . Sir, sir, thou are so leaky
> That we must leave thee to thy sinking, for
> Thy dearest quit thee.   (III.xiii.63–65)

we can be almost certain that Cleopatra, who is on stage, is not supposed to hear his words. We can also be sure that Pisanio's ejaculation in *Cymbeline* (III.v. 104–05) to the absent heroine—

> . . . O Imogen
> Safe mayst thou wander, safe return again!

is not intended to be noticed by Cloten, who is standing beside Pisanio reading a letter. And though possibly

---

13. Twenty of the 129 apostrophes that are delivered in the presence of other actors.

14. In Shakespeare there are fifty-four soliloquies given with other players on the stage. All but one (spoken by Autolycus in *The Winter's Tale*, IV.iv.606–31) are definitely overheard by the other characters. The famous "To be or not to be" soliloquy, delivered by Hamlet with Claudius and Polonius concealed behind the arras curtain and with Ophelia on stage, is, however, a controversial case.

one or two of the other eighteen instances[15] of this kind of thing are not so clearly evident, there are enough definitely valid examples to warrant the conclusion that the unheard apostrophe was an accepted convention on Shakespeare's stage.

15. See *2 Henry VI* (III.i.202–09, III,ii.136–48), *1 Henry VI* (V.i.58–62, V.iv.60–61), *Richard III* (IV.iv.15–16), *The Taming of the Shrew* (I.ii.229), *Richard II* (III.iii.140–41), *A Midsummer Night's Dream* (III.i.109–14), *The Merchant of Venice* (III. ii.111–14, quoted above), *Troilus and Cressida* (I.ii.84–85, V.ii.65), *Macbeth* (IV.i.144, IV.iii.100), *Timon of Athens* (IV.iii.464–75, V.i.53–56), and *Cymbeline* (III.vi.76–79, II.vi. 87–89, quoted above, and IV.ii.33–38).

SEVEN

The Third Type of Aside

☞All previous discussions I have seen assume that stage asides in all Elizabethan plays up to the death of Shakespeare in 1616 are limited to two distinct types: (1) the aside exchanged between actors on the stage out of the hearing of one or more other characters present, and (2) that which is directly addressed to the audience, sometimes given the label *ad spectatores*.

Admittedly, the great majority of the more than 800 asides I detect in the basic texts of Shakespeare do belong under one of the two traditional classifications.[1] But a third distinct group, including nearly 10 percent of the asides in the plays, falls into neither.

On at least seventy-six occasions in twenty of his plays[2] an actor delivers an aside addressed neither to

1. I count 418 asides interchanged by actors and 317 addressed to the audience.
2. For examples not given in this chapter, see *3 Henry VI* (III.ii.30, 34–35, V.vii.21–25), *1 Henry VI* (III.i.177, V.iii.75–76, 81–82), *Richard III* (I.iii.111–12, 118–20, 126, 134, 143–44, and III.ii.121), *Titus Andronicus* (III.i.189–92, IV.ii.6, 8–9, 17, 48), *The Taming of the Shrew* (III.i.50), *Two Gentlemen of Verona* (II.i.126, IV.ii.127–28, V.ii.18, V.iv.32), *Love's Labour's Lost* (IV.iii.52–54, 58–59, 84, 86, 89–90, 93, 97–98), *Henry V* (III.ii.110–11), *Julius Caesar* (II.ii.124–25, 128–29), *As You Like It* (III.v.68–70), *Twelfth Night* (III.iv.318–19), *Troilus and Cressida* (V.ii.33, 45–46, 65, 75, 95–96, 102–03, and V.iv.25–27), *All's Well That Ends Well* (II.iii.105–08, IV.i.35–36, 53, 56, 59, 62, 64–65, 68), *Othello* (II.i.202–04, III.iii.330–33, IV.i.121–22, 130, 146–47), *Timon of Athens*

any of the other players on the stage with him nor to the audience in the playhouse. All of these asides appear to be aimed at another character on the stage[3]— but the words are not intended for his ears or those of any other character. The audience hears them, to be sure, but such asides are apparently not addressed to the house either. An example occurs in *Antony and Cleopatra* (II.vii.87–88) immediately after Menas has been rebuffed by Pompey for suggesting the murder of the triumvirate at sea. Menas assuredly does not intend his general, Pompey, to hear his words:

> For this,
> I'll never follow thy pall'd fortunes more.

and it would only create confusion to address such words directly to the audience with Pompey still in sight, as well as within earshot. The fact that Pompey is still on the open stage with the speaker prevents these two lines from having the effect of an apostrophe.[4] Menas aims an aside at Pompey, but it is not intended for his ears or, as evident in the wording, for the ears of any other character. In like manner, if Aufidius intended this aside, aimed at Coriolanus, for the hearing of another character—

I.ii.113–14, V.i.32–33, 39–42, 50), *Cymbeline* (I.ii.16–17, 21–22, 24–26, I.v.31–32, II.i.25–26, II.iii.82–84), *The Winter's Tale* (I.ii.125–26, IV.iv.652–53, 726), and *The Tempest* (I.ii.438–40, 447–49, II.i.327, III.i.31–32, III.iii.34–36).

3. The sole exceptions are the two occasions on which Suffolk talks to himself (*1 Henry VI*, V.iii.75–76, 184). I list them as asides, in note 2, above, because Margaret, who stands beside Suffolk the while, does not hear his words.

4. The Shakespearean apostrophe, as demonstrated in Chapter 6, above, is always addressed to abstractions, inanimate objects, or characters supposed to be incapable of hearing the words because they are not on the stage or because they are "asleep" or "dead." Pompey, it is clear, fits none of these categories.

> I am glad thou hast set thy mercy and thy
>   honour
> At difference in thee. Out of that I'll work
> Myself a former fortune.
> > (*Coriolanus,* V.iii.200–202)

he would in effect be committing suicide, for standing
near him at the time are Coriolanus himself, Volumnia,
Virgilia, Valeria, and young Marcius, any one of whom
would be expected by the audience to use Aufidius'
words against him on the instant.

Shakespeare uses this neat device as a method of fore-
shadowing, but such an aside could not have been said
directly *ad spectatores.* Still more surely did the actor
playing the part of "Second Lord" in *Cymbeline* intend
to address his aside directly to no one's attention:

> You are a fool granted; therefore your issues,
>   being foolish, do not derogate.
> > (II.i.50–52)

If he allowed Cloten, against whom the aside is directed, to hear these words, his career as a Lord could be
expected to end suddenly. On the other hand, if he
gave them squarely to the audience, some slow-witted
but muscular groundling might feasibly take offense
at being called "fool" and shorten his career as an actor by vaulting the stage rail as "Lucifer" claims to
have done in Middleton's *Black Book* in 1604.[5]

From the wording of such asides it would appear

5. For the often quoted allusion, see A. H. Bullen, ed.,
The Works of Thomas Middleton (8 vols. 1886), VIII, 8. Lucifer's words are—

> . . . And now that I have vaulted up so high
> Above the stage-rails of this earthen globe,
> I must turn actor and join companies, . . .

that while delivering his condemnation[6] the speaker probably faced toward the character on stage against whom they were aimed. To prevent the audience from taking the aside to be the more usual exchange between actors, the deliverer could have changed the tone of his voice, but even without such an expedient the spectators would surely have known from the target character's total lack of reaction to the words that he was not supposed to be aware of the aside. A classic illustration of what the stage business was probably like, and, indeed, should continue to be today in performance, is offered by the well known aside which Iago aims at Cassio (*Othello,* II.i.168–78), the very wording of which assures us that Cassio is too preoccupied with courteous attendance on Desdemona, if not too far removed in stage position, to detect, and thereby react to, Iago's threats:

> He takes her by the palm. Ay, well said, whisper! With as little web as this will I ensnare as great a fly as Cassio. Ay, smile upon her, do! I will gyve thee in thine own courtship. You say true; 'tis so, indeed! If such tricks as these strip you out of your lieutenantry, it had been better you had not kiss'd your three fingers so oft —which now again you are most apt to play the sir in. Very good! well kiss'd! an excellent curtsy! 'Tis so, indeed. Yet again your fingers to your lips? Would they were clyster pipes for your sake! . . .

Though it is possible that Iago risked turning to the audience (surely not to Roderigo!) for the delivery of a few of his words, certainly for most of the speech

---

6. Most asides of this type are derogatory, many being downright threats.

he must have been obliged to look across the stage squarely at Cassio, in order to determine so accurately what the lieutenant and Desdemona were doing, as well as to give his words their most telling dramatic effect.

EIGHT

Stage Settings in the Dialogue

☞ It has always been recognized that Shake-speare's plays, along with those of his contemporary dramatists,[1] abound in lines that establish—and sometimes describe—the setting of the action on the stage.[2] Most of these speeches appear either near the beginning of a new scene or in a scene preceding that to which they apply,[3] some being delivered by professional presenters.[4]

But the consistent stagecraft underlying the convention, in Shakespeare at least, has hitherto been obscured by the practice, I suspect, of limiting the settings to "localization" dialogue—that is, to lines that

1. Almost as consistent as Shakespeare's plays in the employment of the convention are Kyd's *Spanish Tragedy*, Greene's *Friar Bacon*, Jonson's *Every Man in His Humour* and *Eastward Ho*. And there are regular occurrences of the device in all the leading plays of the Elizabethan era, from Lyly to Brome. In contrast, of half a dozen plays written after the Restoration and chosen at random—namely Dryden and Howard's *Indian Queen*, Buckingham's *Rehearsal*, Etherege's *Man of Mode*, Lee's *Rival Queens*, Dryden's *All for Love*, and Otway's *Venice Preserved*—not one line of dialogue is used to establish a stage setting.

2. In Shakespeare, at least, there is no marked fluctuation in frequency of use according to the time of composition.

3. Fully 327 of the 519 total I count, of which sixty-one precede the scene to which they refer.

4. These are usually geographical localizations, like "Verona" in the opening chorus of *Romeo and Juliet*, which merely place the setting rather than attempting to describe it.

place a character geographically by giving the proper name of the locale in which he is supposed to be at the moment. Hence judgments that Shakespeare appears to have followed, consciously, no principles in the matter—and that his practice was not logical or consistent—make the error of confining themselves to geographical settings only, thereby overlooking the main reason for the device.

Actually, geographical localizations are in a notable minority, numbering only about 150 of the more than 500 lines in the plays which help to establish the setting of the action on the stage. An analysis of Shakespeare's settings in bulk unearths a highly systematized pattern of conscious playhouse practice.

Working without the help of scenery changes, on a stage that resembled the interior of an Elizabethan nobleman's dwelling more than anything else, the dramatist seems to have used the greater portion of such dialogue for one of three very practical purposes: (1) to establish exterior settings, without attention to geographic location; (2) to name what the unchanging wall at the rear of the main stage and its inner-space curtains were supposed to represent whenever entering players were to pay attention to them; and (3) to establish part of the stage, at least, as an interior other than a room of a dwelling, most often as a cell.

That an overwhelming majority of the lines should aim primarily at establishing exterior settings is not surprising once we take into account a factor frequently neglected altogether: the appearance, from the audience, of the Elizabethan public stage, even when bare of furniture. With its overhanging "shadow" or "heavens," resembling a ceiling, and two main doors leading into it—together with the hangings (inner-space curtain or curtains) at the rear—the outer platform, as well as the inner space, must have looked to the contemporary audience more like an interior than an exterior. Such a stage, indeed, especially when strewn with rushes of the kind commonly used to cover the floors of Elizabethan homes, would surely have represented to the original spectators the room of a dwelling except on those occasions when the dialogue stipulated otherwise. Thus the dramatist is naturally more preoccupied with inducing his audience to picture exterior settings on a stage which resembles an interior than with establishing geographic locale. Typical in Shakespeare, for example, is the observation of the Soothsayer, in *Julius Caesar,* to Portia,

> Here the street is narrow,   (II.iv.33)

which, it will be noticed, does not identify the street. A similar anonymity[5] applies to all references to streets, and a similar scarcity of proper names is noticeable in allusions to other outdoor localities.[6] Identifications of forests, for instance, are seldom supplied. When the deposed duke opens Act II of *As You Like It* with the memorable speech

> Are not these woods
> More free from peril than the envious court,

he does not include the name of the woods for those spectators who might have forgotten Celia's previous remark (I.iii.109) that her uncle dwelt in "the Forest of Arden." As a matter of fact, the "wood" in an

5. In *2 Henry VI* (IV.viii.1) Cade supplies a proper name when he cries "Up Fish Street," but evidently he refers to some location supposedly offstage.

6. The practice is evident in the plays of Shakespeare's contemporaries as well, particularly in Peele's *Edward I* and *Old Wives Tale,* Greene's *Orlando Furioso,* Kyd's *Spanish Tragedy,* Dekker's *Old Fortunatus,* Heywood's *Woman Killed with Kindness* and *Fair Maid of the West,* and Beaumont and Fletcher's *Philaster.*

earlier play, *The Two Gentlemen of Verona,* is not
named at all. Because common nouns like "field,"
"park," and "bush" in *Love's Labour's Lost* do not
establish a setting geographically, some dismay has
been expressed at what is considered to be the vague-
ness of reference to place running through that play.
Yet even a monologue as indefinite about location as
that of Cinna the poet, near the beginning of Act III,
scene iii, in *Julius Caesar,*

> I have no will to wander forth of doors,
> Yet something leads me forth,

informs the audience admirably that Cinna is standing somewhere outdoors, where he is more vulnerable
to the onrush of the lynching party unleashed by the
oratory of Antony.

Even less obtrusive are lines which, though they establish or stress exterior settings effectively, tell nothing whatever about the location of the character.
These simply supply the information that he is now
going somewhere, as, for example, when Petruchio, in
The Taming of the Shrew, says to Katherine,

> Come on, a God's name! once more toward
> our father's.   (IV.v.1)

Speeches of this kind, "en route" lines, as it were, are
not casual either, for they appear in twelve of Shakespeare's plays.[7] Moreover, like the more common type
of dialogue that establishes exterior settings, thirteen

7. The other en route lines are in *The Two Gentlemen of
Verona* (IV.i.16–19); *Richard III* (I.i.43–45, I.ii.29–30, V.ii.
10–13); *Richard II* (V.i.1–6); *Twelfth Night* (II.ii.1–4); *The
Merry Wives of Windsor* (II.i.33–34); *Troilus and Cressida*
(V.i.74–75); *Measure for Measure* (I.ii.117–18); *All's Well
That Ends Well* (V.i.27–29); *Timon of Athens* (V.i.1–2); *Cym-
beline* (III.iv.1–2, III.v.1, III.vi.4–6, 58–59, and IV.i.1–2); *The
Tempest* (III.iii.1–2).

of the eighteen en route lines appear near the beginning of a scene. And, possibly because characters in
the act of entering can more readily give the impression of being on the move, the other five examples are
spoken by newcomers joining a scene already in prog-
ress. Despite their naturalness, en route lines not only
imply that the enterer is on the move, but, since a
player could hardly be thought of as traveling in a
room, they tell the audience he is supposed to be outside on an exterior setting. Hence the en route line
serves the same purpose as speeches concerning a present location, which include hint words like "street,"
"woods," and "forth of doors."

A second consistent function of such dialogue,
which, though frequently mentioned, has heretofore remained unexplored, is to point out to the audience
what the permenent front wall of the tiring house represents,[8] whenever such information becomes significant to the action. As has often been observed, numerous lines in the plays refer to the "walls" of cities or
the "gates," sometimes without including the name of
the city. Not so plentiful but equally purposeful are
references to the outside of private dwellings. Some
concern the doors of houses, as that given in *The
Comedy of Errors* by Antipholus to Dromio,

> But soft! my door is lock'd.   (III.i.30)

For the outside of castles, on the other hand, there is
no mention of "doors," so that in *Richard II* (III.iii.32)
Bolingbroke identifies Flint by referring to its "rude
ribs." And, as everyone recalls, on the exterior of Inverness (*Macbeth* I.vi.1–10) the dramatist expends
some of his most beautiful poetry. Regardless of

---

8. Only Peele's *David and Bethsabe* and Jonson's *Every Man
in His Humour* seem to identify the tiring-house wall as consistently as does Shakespeare.

method, however, all dialogue of this type accomplishes the highly practical purpose of telling the audience what structure is supposed to be confronting them in a particular scene. Moreover, the majority of such lines occur soon after an entrance, when characters are most likely to pay heed to the background of their surroundings.

An examination of such dialogue in all the plays further demonstrates how conscious the dramatist always must have been of the appearance of the stage for which he wrote. The front wall of the tiring house, along with its inner-space curtains, retains the same appearance from scene to scene, if not from play to play. As soon as entering actors direct attention to this wall, Shakespeare appears to have reasoned, the audience wants to be told what it represents. Is it supposed to be the entrance to a city? In the preceding scene, perhaps, it has represented the outside of a castle. Or, if the dialogue in that scene gave no identification, the audience may have thought of the wall, with its hangings, as the rear of a room. Is it supposed to be the front of a house? Or is part of the wall—the inner-space curtain of either level—not intended to be taken as the hangings at the back of a room in this scene, but, rather, as the entrance to some kind of cell? If the backing of the platform stage were used for the same thing throughout a play, of course, speeches identifying it would have less point. But in the rear of Shakespeare's platform stage the curtains, as well as the wall, go unnamed only until the players begin paying attention to them. Then the dialogue consistently identifies them as soon as possible—as the "gates" of a city, for instance, or the "door" of a house or the "mouth" of a cell. The dramatist must also have been aware that whenever he identified the backing of the outer platform as the front of an enclosure, at the same time he was effectively establishing, by implication, the platform itself as an exterior setting.

The appearance of the Elizabethan public stage is also responsible, no doubt, for the comparatively small number of lines in Shakespeare (fifty-eight compared to the 256 connoting exteriors) that establish the setting as an interior. And, as has been noted, because the stage must have resembled the inside of an upper-class dwelling more than anything else, hardly any of these lines concern "rooms"[9] but, rather, concentrate on identifying the second kind of interior which the dramatist most regularly employed, namely the cell, of either the prison or the friar variety.[10] Richard II's description of his whereabouts, "This prison where I live" (V.v.2), is typical, for every time a character is in what is supposed to be a prison, the dialogue says so.[11] And the other type of cell seems invariably to have required like identification.

9. Very rare indeed are the four successive identifications of the interior of a dwelling (the palace of Theseus) in *A Midsummer Night's Dream* (V.i.394–427), where Puck and Oberon between them use the word "house" thrice and "palace" once. Possibly the dramatist was attempting to dissociate the entering fairies from the woodland setting in which they had invariably appeared up to this point in the action.

10. In Greene's *Friar Bacon*, too, the philosopher's "cell" is named as such whenever it is supposed to be part of the stage setting.

11. See, for example, *1 Henry VI*, II.v.57 ("within a loathsome dungeon"); *King John*, IV.i.17 ("so I were out of prison"); and *Measure for Measure*, II.iii.5 ("here in the prison").

Shakespeare's Playhouse Practice

Whenever Friar Laurence, in *Romeo and Juliet,* for example, appears in his cell, the dialogue labels the setting as such,[12] though it may fail to identify, say, a room in the house of Capulet. The stage looked like a room but evidently not like a cell, any more than like an exterior.

12. *Romeo and Juliet,* II.ii.190–91, II.v.70–79, III.ii.140–41, III.v.233–35. All four examples end scenes immediately preceding those in which the friar appears in his cell.

NINE

Time Signals

☞ Of the numerous references to time in Shakespeare's dialogue,[1] only those concerning the
present seem to have been made necessary by the
physical aspects of the public playhouse.[2] As in the
modern theater, references to time already elapsed[3]
are normally expository,[4] and those to some time in
the future[5] are almost always dramatic, creating sus-
pense, or anticipation.[6] On the other hand, the overwhelming majority of references to time in the present clearly serve the dramaturgical purpose of either

1. I count a total of 556.

2. How Shakespeare managed to foreshorten time is not
part of this study.

3. There are only thirty-eight in the plays.

4. For example: "within these five hours Hastings lived"
(*Richard III*, III.vi.8); "Even now, even here, not half an hour
since" (*The Comedy of Errors*, II.ii.14); "he hath known you
but three days, and already you are no stranger" (*Twelfth
Night*, I.iv.3–4); "after seven years siege yet Troy walls
stand" (*Troilus and Cressida*, I.iii.12); "this twenty years, /
This rock, and these demesnes, have been my world" (*Cym-
line*, III.iii.69–70).

5. They total 116.

6. For example: "My woes end likewise with the evening
sun" (*The Comedy of Errors*, I.i.27); "here are your parts
. . . con them by tomorrow night, and meet me in the palace wood, a mile without the town, by moon-light. There
will we rehearse" (*A Midsummer Night's Dream*, I.ii.101–05);
"Three thousand ducats for three months, and Antonio
bound" (*The Merchant of Venice*, I.iii.9–10); "To-morrow
are to die Claudio and Barnardine" (*Measure for Measure*,
IV.ii.7–8); "Ride you this afternoon?" (*Macbeth*, III.i.19).

establishing darkness on the open-air, afternoon stage or re-establishing daylight on a stage which has been effectively "darkened" previously.

On occasion the dramatist attempted to establish the time of day of the action with clock-hour references.[7] But for this purpose[8] they soon proved valueless—in some cases, actually detrimental. A player could hardly resort to stipulating, unnaturally, "A.M." or "P.M." Therefore, Shakespeare was obliged to write three speeches in *Richard III* (III.ii.4-6) for only one time signal, the first two being:

> *Hastings.* What is't o'clock?
> *Messenger.* Upon the stroke of four.

The natural inference is that he referred to the middle of the afternoon. Especially would this apply to an audience viewing the actual scene at some time between 3:00 and 4:00 P.M., in the dramatist's open-air playhouse. Hence to prevent confusion the dramatist caused Hastings to say immediately,

> Cannot my Lord Stanley sleep these tedious nights?

Indeed, the next time he uses "four" to express time in this play, the dramatist obviates any confusion about the matter by preceding the clock hour with a direct allusion to morning:

> *Richmond.* How far into the morning is it, lords?

---

7. There are thirty-eight altogether.

8. A few clock-hour references merely express mood, usually impatience. For example: "and from nine to twelve / Is three long hours, yet she is not come" (*Romeo and Juliet*, II.v.10-11); "How say you now, is it not past two o'clock? And here much Orlando" (*As You Like It*, IV.iii.1-2); " 'Tis the ninth hour o'th'morn" (*Cymbeline*, IV.ii.30).

Time Signals

> *Lords.* Upon the stroke of four.
>
> (V.iii.235-36)

By this point in the performance (V.iii) it is probably
very near that hour in the afternoon. If Prince Hal's
line to Poins in *1 Henry IV* (II.iv.104-07),

> I am now of all humours that have showed
>   themselves humours since the old days of
>   goodman Adam to the pupil age of this pres-
>   ent twelve o'clock at midnight,

had not been tagged at the end with the clarifying
term "midnight," an afternoon audience in a roofless
playhouse would surely have taken "twelve o'clock"
as referring to noon. By the time Shakespeare had
written *Julius Caesar* he apparently decided to employ
clock-hour references very seldom, for he spreads only
ten examples of them through all the rest of his plays.[9]
   Since the dramatist's chief reason for using time signals was to establish darkness on his open-air, afternoon stage quickly and effectively, it is not at all surprising to discover that the most numerous signals in
the plays are those which refer to night.[10] Moreover,
this type appears in every play that features scenes
supposed to take place after dark.[11] In as early a play
as *2 Henry VI*, for illustration, Bolingbroke informs

   9. One in *As You Like It*, one in *Hamlet*, two in *The Merry
Wives of Windsor*, one in *All's Well That Ends Well*, one in
Othello, one in *Timon of Athens*, two in *Cymbeline*, and one
in *The Tempest*. In *Julius Caesar*, on the other hand, there are
four examples.
   10. Fully 142.
   11. The three plays with most references to night are *A Midsummer Night's Dream* (twenty-seven), *The Merchant of Venice* (twenty-four), and *Romeo and Juliet* (ten). The only plays
containing no such time signals are *3 Henry VI*, *The Comedy
of Errors*, *Titus Andronicus*, *The Taming of the Shrew*, *Love's
Labour's Lost*, *Richard II*, *Coriolanus*, *Timon of Athens*, and
The Tempest.

the audience that it is supposed to be night by saying to the Duchess of Gloucester,

> Patience, good lady; wizards know their times.
> Deep night, dark night, the silent of the
> night, . . .   (I.iv.18–19)

When Duncan (*Macbeth,* I.vi.25) says to Lady Macbeth, in much more natural style,

> . . . We are your guest to-night,

he emphasizes the "darkness" already established by the display of the "torches" referred to in the initial stage direction of the scene.[12] Time and again, as we should expect, the dramatist seems to be at some pains to make his allusions to darkness agreeable as well as effective, as in the poetic utterance of Lorenzo to Jessica in the first scene of Act V in *The Merchant of Venice* and in the vivid imagery of Kent's speech to King Lear at III.ii.42–45. Moreover, many night allusions omit the term *night* from their wording altogether. In *The Two Gentlemen of Verona,* for instance, Eglamour announces the approach of darkness by referring to the sunset (V.v.1), and in *A Midsummer Night's Dream,* a play necessarily abounding in allusions to night,[13] Oberon performs a similar duty with a neat reference to the "moonlight" (II.i.60). But how subtle the dramatist can become in maintaining the illusion of darkness, after it has been established by more direct verbal signals, is well illustrated in this exchange of lines from *Much Ado About Nothing:*

---

12. Duncan's time signal may be to re-establish a "night" possibly weakened somewhat by the vivid description of Inverness Castle delivered by himself and Banquo earlier in the scene.

13. See note 11, above.

> *Borachio.* Conrade, I say!
> *Conrade.* Here, man. I am at thy elbow.
> (III.iii.104–05)

We do not have to perceive Borachio peering and grop-
ing for his companion to get the effect of the dialogue.
And after darkness has been established in the first
scene of *Othello,* the dramatist has Roderigo give this
crafty reminder through the wording of his speech to
Brabantio,

> Most reverend signior, do you know my
> voice?   (I.i.93)

instead of, say, "do you recognize my face?" In *The
Merchant of Venice* (V.i.40–48) the illusion of darkness in a scene where night has been firmly established in the first twenty lines is cleverly prolonged
by this dialogue:

> *Lorenzo.* Who calls?
> *Launcelot.* Sola! Did you see Master Lorenzo
>   and Mistress Lorenzo? Sola, sola!
> *Lorenzo.* Leave holloaing, man! Here.
> *Launcelot.* Sola! Where? where?
> *Lorenzo.* Here!
> *Launcelot.* Tell him there's a post come from
>   my master, with his horn full of good news.
>   My master will be here ere morning.

Launcelot's "Tell him," along with the more obvious
indications in his speech, convinces the audience that
it is too dark for the clown to see Lorenzo's face.

The ever-present glare of daylight in his open-air
playhouse seems to have obliged the dramatist to pre-
serve the "darkness" of his night scenes by scattering
signals through them generously. Hence in scene iii,
Act V of *Richard III* the players are given ten references to night. In scene i, Act V of *The Merchant of*

Venice twenty such time signals are provided, though some, admittedly, are for purposes other than merely darkening the stage. And when the stage is supposed to be in darkness beyond one scene, the dramatist preserves the illusion of night by continuing to use signals from scene to scene, as though he suspected that to some spectators a cleared stage might signify the end of darkness. Thus in *A Midsummer Night's Dream,* a play with four successive scenes enacted at night, Act II, scene i contains such signals as "to night," "wanderer of the night," "by moonlight," "our moonlight revels," "the opportunity of night," and "in the night";[14] scene ii continues with "The clamorous owl, that nightly hoots," "good night," "tarry for the comfort of the day," "Night and silence!", and "wilt thou darkling leave me?";[15] Act III, scene i, perhaps because it is necessary to explain how the rustics could have read their play lines and how everyone could have seen Bottom's new head so clearly, includes only the single allusion—"The moon, methinks, looks with a wat'ry eye" (III.i.203); but scene ii reverts to stronger time signals with "night rule," "yonder Venus," "Dark night," "Since night," "by night," "overcast the night," "night's swift dragons," "black browed night," "ere day," "art thou bragging to the stars," and "O weary night, O long and tedious night."[16] In these four scenes the dramatist employed so many night signals that we can almost detect him parodying himself when he has Bottom, as "Pyramus," cry out,

> O grim-look'd night! O night with hue so
> black!

14. II.i.18, 43, 60, 141, 217, 222.
15. II.ii.6, 19, 38, 70, 86.
16. III.ii.5, 61, 177, 275, 283, 355, 379, 387, 395, 407, 431.

> O night, which ever art when day is not!
> O night, O night! alack, alack, alack . . .
>
> (V.i.171-73)

As his art matured, however, the dramatist seems to have discovered that he could darken his stage sufficiently with fewer allusions to night. By the time he wrote *King Lear,* in fact, he apparently found that a single night signal, if placed at the beginning of a scene, was sometimes enough to establish darkness, as in Oswald's greeting to Kent opening scene ii of Act II.

But Shakespeare seems to have taken as great pains to establish daylight on his stage. Quite frequent, for instance, are his allusions to morning,[17] many of which are direct indeed.[18] As with night signals, however, several references accomplish the same end without actually including the word "morning." Hence Orleans refers to the sunrise indirectly by saying to his French companions in *Henry V,*

> The sun doth gild our armour. . . .
>
> (IV.ii.1)

Even more indirect is Hero, in *Much Ado About Nothing,* when she says,

> Good Ursula, wake my cousin Beatrice and
>   desire her to rise.   (III.iv.1-2)

Yet both her line and that of Orleans tell the audience adequately that the scenes which they open are to be played in what is supposedly early morning. Paris, in *Troilus and Cressida* (IV.i.34), is made to achieve the same result merely by the use of the adverb "early,"

17. Fifty are distributed through the plays.
18. See, for example, *Richard III*, V.iii.235; *Henry V,* IV.i. 87-88; *Othello*, II.iii.384-85.

but even more subtle is the Queen in *Cymbeline,* who opens a scene (I.v) with

> Whiles yet the dew's on the ground, gather
> those flowers.

Now for spectators viewing these plays in broad daylight it may seem strange that the dramatist should have to establish the fact that it is morning at all. But the reason becomes clear upon the discovery that morning time signals usually follow night scenes. Apparently early in his career Shakespeare learned how very successful his allusions to night were in darkening the stage, and how lasting the impression was on his audience. Thus in *1 Henry VI* (a very early play) he has Bedford open a new scene (II.ii) with the time signal,

> The day begins to break and night is fled,
> Whose pitchy mantle overveil'd the earth,

because the previous scene showed the English, under Talbot, making a surprise attack on the French, an attack so unexpected, indeed, that the audience caught a glimpse of some French leaders running across the stage in their nightshirts. In *1 Henry IV* the King opens a scene (V.i) with the description to his men,

> How bloodily the sun begins to peer
> Above yon busky hill! The day looks pale
> At his distemp-rature,

probably, among other purposes, to offset the effect of the night time signals in the two previous scenes. Even in the last play that features night scenes, *Cymbeline,*[19] Shakespeare still uses the same device.

---

19. *The Winter's Tale* has one short night scene of little consequence, and *The Tempest* has none.

Time Signals

Early in the scene (II.iii.10–11) which follows the one that featured Imogen asleep in her bed, there appears the short, but illuminating dialogue:

> *Cloten.* . . . It's almost morning, is't not?
> *First Lord.* Day, my lord,

which permits the audience to accept a daylight stage once more.

But there seems to have been a method both more economical and more natural than allusions to morning whereby the dramatist could re-establish daylight on the stage. This was through the use of the unobtrusive, but very effective, salutation "good morrow."[20] The employment of any salutation would be limited, of course, to only the points in the action where a player enters an occupied stage. But there can be little doubt about the meaning of "good morrow": that it always signifies morning is clearly pointed out in some of the lines.[21] Moreover, that the salutation is not to be used after noontime is clearly established by Mercutio's correcting the Nurse in *Romeo and Juliet* (II.iv.115–19):

> *Nurse.* God ye good morrow, gentlemen.
> *Mercutio.* God ye good-den, fair gentlewoman.

20. Forty-one times during the plays one character greets another with "good morrow": there are six examples in *Richard III*, one in *The Taming of the Shrew*, two in *The Two Gentlemen of Verona*, one in *Love's Labour's Lost*, one in *Romeo and Juliet*, one in *A Midsummer Night's Dream*, one in *King John*, one in *The Merchant of Venice*, three in *1 Henry IV*, five in *2 Henry IV*, four in *Much Ado About Nothing*, three in *Henry V*, two in *As You Like It*, one in *Twelfth Night*, three in *The Merry Wives of Windsor*, two in *Troilus and Cressida*, one in *All's Well That Ends Well*, one in *Measure for Measure*, and two in *Cymbeline*.

21. For example, *Richard III*, III.ii.35–36, III.iv.22–23; *Romeo and Juliet*, I.i.167–68; *1 Henry IV*, II.iv.572–74.

> *Nurse.* Is it good-den?
> *Mercutio.* 'Tis no less, I tell ye; for the bawdy
>   hand of the dial is now upon the prick of
>   noon.

Mercutio also informs us here that "good den," and its variations, always means noon or afternoon, but this greeting is employed not nearly so often in the plays[22] as "good morrow." Possibly the dramatist felt he could dispel the "darkness" of a previous night scene more effectively, as well as more naturally, with an allusion to morning rather than to afternoon.

22. In contrast to the forty-one examples of "good morrow" (see note 20, above), there are but six instances of "good den."

TEN

Exit Cues

☞Important to an understanding of the efficiency of Shakespeare's playhouse practice are the devices he consistently employed to get the players off the stage at the right time. Practically every exit occurring in the plays is denoted in the dialogue, either through an announcement from the exiter himself, a request or command from another character, or a rhyme tag at the end of the exiter's speech. Dramatically, to be sure, many of the devices serve to give shape and direction to the plays and sometimes, through the information they convey, to set up the supposed locale of later scenes, as do the several exit announcements in *Romeo and Juliet* which stipulate the next setting as the Friar's cell. But for the existence in the plays of as many as 1540 exit signals, many of which are undramatic, there can be only two possible dramaturgical explanations: first, that they were used for the benefit of the spectators, to prepare them for the departure of a character from the stage, or second, that they were for the sake of the actor, to give him his cue for leaving the stage at the proper moment. And the evidence seems to point to the conclusion that though such devices may have helped to grace exits or to serve other dramatic purposes, all appear to have functioned also as exit cues—cues vital to the success of performances given on a stage bare of scenery by a company of actors who played repertory.

In nearly every play Shakespeare has his characters forecast some of their exits by making announcements of their intention to leave the stage.[1] The type in danger of being most obtrusive, the announcement made directly to the audience, is fortunately in the minority.[2] Most of these, of course, are delivered in soliloquy form by players alone on stage, like Prospero's

> I'll to my book;
> For yet ere supper time must I perform
> Much business appertaining
> > (*The Tempest,* III.i.94–96)

which is not so obtrusive as some others of the type because it also tells the audience what Prospero is about to do, sets the time of the action, and creates some anticipation of his future behavior. Perhaps slightly less obvious as a class are exit announcements given in apostrophes, as is Iden's address to the body of the fallen Cade in *2 Henry VI:*

> Hence will I drag thee headlong by the heels.
> > (IV.x.86)

But these appear in fewer than one third of the plays,[3] only five occurring in dramas later than *A Midsummer Night's Dream,*[4] which would seem to indicate that the

1. The only plays containing fewer than half a dozen exit announcements are *Hamlet, Julius Caesar, Timon of Athens, 2 Henry IV, Othello,* and *King John.* The play having the greatest number is *The Merry Wives of Windsor,* with 22.

2. Only 64 of the total 379 announcements.

3. Only ten, seven of which have but one example each: *Titus Andronicus, Romeo and Juliet, Troilus and Cressida, Macbeth, Antony and Cleopatra, Cymbeline,* and *The Winter's Tale.* The three plays with more than one apostrophe announcement are *2 Henry VI* (with two), *3 Henry VI* (with five), and *A Midsummer Night's Dream* (with five).

4. The other four appear in *Troilus and Cressida,* V.vi.30–31 (Hector to "one in armour"); *Antony and Cleopatra,* III.xiii.65 (Enobarbus to Antony, who is off stage); *Cymbeline,* IV.i.26

playwright quickly tired of the device. By and large, exit announcers direct their speech to other characters on stage. And most of these announcements, like those to the audience, are worded simply, as in Cardinal Beufort's announcement to his companions in *2 Henry VI*:

> I'll to the Duke of Suffolk presently
> (I.i.171)

which, as with the announcement of Prospero given above, also creates anticipation in the audience.

Though, as we should expect, most announcements concern the exit of the announcer alone, a small group includes other characters. Thus, in *The Winter's Tale,* Hermione announces to her husband her intention of departing with Polixenes by saying,

> If you would seek us,
> We are yours i'th'garden. Shall's attend you
> there?   (I.ii.177-78)

which is natural enough in its wording. Accomplishing the same purpose, but more clumsily, are exit announcements that come in bunches. How crude these are is clearly illustrated in an example from the very early *3 Henry VI,* where four noblemen in succession are made to announce exits to their King:

> *York.* Farewell, my gracious lord. I'll to my
>   castle.
> *Warwick.* And I'll keep London with my sol-
>   diers.
> *Norfolk.* And I to Norfolk with my followers.
> *Montague.* And I unto the sea, from whence I
>   came.   (I.i.206-09)

(Cloten to his drawn sword); and *The Winter's Tale*, III.iii.53-58 (Antigonus to the infant Perdita).

Shakespeare's Playhouse Practice

The two players left on stage (Henry and Exeter) also announce their intention of exiting, but the entering Queen prevents them from doing so. Fortunately Shakespeare seems to have very soon wearied of herding his players off the stage by so obvious a method, so that after *Richard II*[5] never do more than two exit announcements occur in succession, and most of these coupled announcements of later date are more polished than the blunt statements above.

But whatever the method or the dramatic by-product, exit announcements are really not required by the audience. An actor should not have to explain his exits, except on those rare occasions when it becomes dramatically important to do so, any more than he should have to justify his entrances. He is not even obliged to inform spectators (either directly or through another player) of his intention of leaving the stage. The fact that he leaves is normally sufficient. He may grace his exit, as many actors do, with stage business or verbal intonation, but even these are not essential. On the modern stage, of course, some exits are achieved by closing front curtains or by blackouts, but these devices are usually resorted to only at the ends of scenes or acts. The majority of modern exits usually are not preceded by any verbal indication.

Much more numerous than announcements are requests to exit.[6] In every play, exit requests outnumber announcements by a substantial margin, and to the close of his career the dramatist continued to use the

5. The only two really late examples are in *Cymbeline* (V.iv.1–2) and *The Tempest* (III.iii.102–03).
6. I count 1109. A fairly late play, *The Merry Wives of Windsor,* leads the list with 54 examples. However, the very early *Richard III* has 53 requests. Another mature play, *Julius Caesar,* contains the smallest number, 11. But the early *Titus Andronicus* has only 15 requests.

device without significant change in frequency.[7] That
the request should be preferable is not surprising,
since, though it does not lend itself as well as the announcement to dramatic effect, it is far less obtrusive,
and it is much more practicable at the same time.
Thus York, in *2 Henry VI* (I.iv.83), can include Buckingham, his other followers, and himself in the undramatic but very effective brief command, "Away!"—a
simple imperative frequently used by the dramatist to
clear the stage of everyone at once. Impressive as evidence that requests are cues are those which seem to
stipulate two separate passageways for one general
exit. For illustration, two individual requests are necessary in *Troilus and Cressida* to indicate both a main
exit door and the inner space:

> *Ulysses* (to Troilus concerning Diomedes).
>   Follow his torch; he goes to Calchas' tent.
>   I'll keep you company.
> *Troilus.* Sweet sir, you honour me.
> *Hector.* And so good night.
> *Achilles.* Come, come, enter my tent.
>   (V.i.92–94)

The *"Exeunt"* that follows apparently indicates that
Ulysses and Troilus depart through one of the main
doorways (on the way to Calchas' tent), and that Hector and Achilles leave the outer stage through the inner-space curtain (into Achilles' tent). In *Coriolanus*
(I.vii.6–7), Lartius pauses to send a lieutenant into the
inner space before ordering his follower to accompany
him through a main exit:

---

7. There are 564 in the first eighteen plays, compared with
545 in the remaining seventeen. The first play, *2 Henry VI,*
uses 42 exit requests, but the late *Cymbeline* has 41.

> Hence, and shut your gates upon's.
> Our guider, come; to th' Roman camp con-
> duct us.

Thus Shakespeare seems to be reminding his players to leave in different directions by including the instruction, undramatic as it may be, in their exit cue.

But even more apparently for the benefit of the exiters alone are the frequent requests which carefully stipulate who is supposed to leave the stage first, and so on. In some of these the speaker merely asks the others on stage to follow him off. Marcius, in *Coriolanus* (I.i.254–55), makes clear not only that he is sarcastic to the citizens but also that he is to precede them off the stage, when he says

> Worshipful mutiners,
> Your valour puts well forth. Pray follow.

And the clown in *The Winter's Tale* (V.ii.186–88), accompanied by his father, boasts to Autolycus:

> Hark! the kings and the princes, our kindred,
> are going to see the Queen's picture. Come,
> follow us. We'll be thy good masters.

The wording of this speech illustrates an important characteristic of the exit request: the masters normally precede their inferiors off the stage. On occasion, however, for dramatic purposes, Shakespeare lets the characters cast normal precedence aside. For example, Talbot, in *1 Henry VI* (IV.v.54–55), is permitted to show his admiration for a worthy son by wording an exit request:

> Come, side by side together live and die,
> And soul with soul from France to heaven
> fly!

Exit Cues

And in *Much Ado About Nothing,* the gratitude of
Don Pedro to his host temporarily equalizes their so-
cial standing for an exit:

> *Leonato.* Please it your Grace lead on?
> *Don Pedro.* Your hand, Leonato. We will go
> together.   (I.i.160–62)

With what meticulous care Shakespeare usually followed the convention of exit precedence according to
rank, however, is more clearly demonstrated by Lady
Macbeth's dramatic command to her dinner guests
when she hurries them off the stage with,

> At once, good night.
> Stand not upon the order of your going,
> But go at once.   (*Macbeth,* III.iv.118–20)

By dispensing with the normal ceremonious exit by
rank, she gives herself quicker opportunity to soothe
the overwrought nerves of her husband. Moreover, for
the great majority of Shakespearean exits (1045 of
1109), rank determines not only who leaves the stage
first, but also who gives the original exit request. The
dramatist does allow some inferiors to do the requesting, to establish dramatically that they hold the upper
hand temporarily in the action. Hence in *3 Henry VI*
(III.i.97–98), a keeper loyal to the usurping King,
York, shows his temerity by commanding his anointed
King, Henry, to exit with him. An outlaw in *The Two
Gentlemen of Verona* (V.iii.12–14) requests the Countess Silvia to depart because she happens to be his cap-
tive at the moment. And the position of self-appointed
advisers assumed by Nurse and Friar in *Romeo and
Juliet* is dramatically established by their giving exit
commands to their younger superiors.[8] In *Much Ado*

8. Thrice the Nurse gives exit requests to Juliet (I.v.146–47,

About Nothing, the convention appears to be broken
three times (I.i.160, II.iii.218, and IV.i.252–55) for
dramatic effect, twice by Leonato and once by Friar
Francis. Both of Leonato's requests to Don Pedro em-
phasize that he is speaking in the role of host, and the
Friar's request to Leonato and Hero is one of religious
solace, needed after the scene at the wedding altar.
But for all practical purposes, Shakespeare adheres
very closely to the convention that gives the highest
in rank the privilege of delivering the exit request. Indeed, fully eleven of his plays[9] contain not a single instance of a request given by an inferior. Thus the exit
requests, though for the most part they are not dramatic, appear natural enough to screen the fact that they
are cues to the exiters. An Elizabethan audience would
expect those higher in rank to order their inferiors off
the stage. Since the parts of superiors in rank were
most often played by the leading actors, moreover,
the convention must have assured further that the less
competent apprentice actors and hirelings would leave
the stage at the proper time.

Yet probably the strongest single proof that the device was an exit cue is that nearly all exit requests in
Shakespeare specify exactly who is to make the departure. Most frequently, of course, this is accomplished
merely by supplementing the lines one player is delivering directly to another with the request. But whenever there might be a question about the identity of
exiters, the dialogue singles them out. Hence the

II.v.79, and III.ii.138). Thrice also the Friar gives exit orders to
his superiors: once to the two lovers (II.vi.35–37), once to Romeo alone (III.iii.166–72), and once to the two elder Capulets
and Count Paris (IV.v.91–92).

9. *A Midsummer Night's Dream, 1 Henry IV, Julius Caesar,
Twelfth Night, Hamlet, The Merry Wives of Windsor, Measure
for Measure, Othello, King Lear, Timon of Athens,* and *The
Tempest.*

Queen in *2 Henry VI* (I.iii.43) indicates through the
wording of her command to the petitioners—"Away,
base cullions! Suffolk, let them go"—not only that the
suitors are to leave the stage, but also that Suffolk,
the only other occupant, is not to leave with them.
And for further assurance on the point, it may be, the
petitioners themselves add, "Come, let's be gone."
More smoothly, and with more dramatic import, the
dramatist has Henry IV word an exit request to include everyone on the stage at the time but Prince Hal
and himself:

> Lords, give us leave. The Prince of Wales and I
> Must have some private conference; but be
>   near at hand,
> For we shall presently have need of you.
>   (*1 Henry IV,* III.ii.1-3)

and in the next play more briefly accomplishes the
same end by having the King again say to the lords,
about Prince Hal and himself, "Depart the chamber,
leave us here alone" (*2 Henry IV,* IV.v.91). And Henry
V is made to clear the stage rather undramatically of
everyone but himself and Katherine by calling each of
the exiters by name:

> Go, uncle Exeter,
> And brother Clarence, and you brother
>   Gloucester,
> Warwick, and Huntingdon—go with the
>   King; . . .   (*Henry V,* V.ii.83-85)

which very likely is also a stipulation to exit according to rank. Moreover, the dozen or so requests which
are indefinite about the identity of the exiters all follow the one pattern. For the Duke's request in *The
Comedy of Errors* (V.i.280)—"Go call the Abbess
hither"—the marginal notation in the Folio indicates
the exiter to be a supernumerary: *"Exit one to the*

Shakespeare's Playhouse Practice

Abess." Some requests, however, have no accompanying marginal notations in the basic text. Such is Henry V's command (I.ii.221)—"Call in the messengers sent from the Dauphin"—which is not accompanied by an "Exit" in the Folio text. The French King in *All's Well That Ends Well* is obscure on four separate occasions about who is to fetch other characters on to the stage for him,[10] and in *Cymbeline* (III.v.34–35) occurs a strange instance when the King asks someone to fetch Imogen by saying,

> Call her before us, for
> We have been too slight in sufferance,

which is accompanied by no "Exit" in the margin. Six lines later, nevertheless, a notation reads: *"Enter a Messenger"*—evidently the actor who sought Imogen, for the King says to him,

> Where is she, sir? How
> Can her contempt be answer'd?   (41–42)

It is impossible to determine, of course, whether omissions of exit notations were in such instances deliberate or accidental. A close examination of all the examples, however, leads to the conclusion that exit requests are indefinite only when an order is given to fetch a newcomer on to the stage. It is possible that in some cases, at least, the attendant never really left the stage but merely signaled offstage for the newcomer to enter.

The fact remains that whenever an exiter is to remain off the stage for a reasonable period of time, his identity is specified in the exit request and the specification serves no dramatic purpose. Now no audience needs such careful identification. Spectators, surely,

10. At II.iii.52 and V.iii.25–27, 152, 204.

should be satisfied merely with a general request followed by an exit. Apparently, then, it is the actor involved in the exit who needs specification of his identity, as a cue to inform him exactly when he is supposed to leave the stage.

But why should Shakespeare's players have needed cues worded so obviously as the announcement and the request? For one thing, only lines can be prompted with any degree of safety, for whatever the prompter calls out from his box, the actor is conditioned to repeat, word for word. Hence no prompter (Elizabethan or modern) can possibly say "Exit" or "Leave the stage," without risking the absurd mishap of being echoed on the stage by the very player he is attempting to rescue. The same, incidentally, holds true for attempts to prompt stage business, a good reason for attaching little significance to the few imperatives that have crept into the marginal directions of the basic texts.

The real reason Shakespeare's players required such obvious cues for their exits probably lies in a fact too often forgotten: his company played repertory. Unlike lines, exits are not memorized verbally. On the contrary, they must be coupled kinesthetically with lines, cues, and especially with stage groupings. Exits are easy enough to learn for an actor who plays a part in but one play over a period of time. In fact, a few rehearsals ordinarily will train him to leave the stage after a specific line and during a particular grouping of the others on stage with him.[11] But for an actor who has to perform a half dozen or more different plays at alternate performances (as in repertory), the problem becomes more acute.

11. Even so, I have witnessed amateur players begin to make a false exit at a point in the play when personnel and grouping duplicated those which had marked a previous exit.

Shakespeare's Playhouse Practice

Would not the identical problem face the members of modern repertory companies? I think not. In a modern repertory company (few remain in the United States) the personnel normally differs from play to play. But much more to the point, the scenery changes. The Shakespearean stage setting, as well as the personnel of the principal parts, always remained essentially the same. Say that at one exit a Shakespearean actor found himself leaving the bare outer platform stage from a position down left, at a time when the other players on stage were up center and down right, respectively. Whenever this exiter found himself on stage again with two actors (especially the same two) in these positions, he might well be urged to exit whether he was supposed to or not. A modern actor, on the other hand, might learn to exit from, say, a drawing-room set, with actor B near the "center hallway door" (up center) and C in front of the "fireplace" (down right). In a later scene, this time a bedroom set, the same player might find himself on stage with B and C holding the same relative positions they had at the time of his former exit. But this time B stands at the "head of the bed" (though up center again), and C stands in front of a "window" (though down right again). Thus the change of scenery would prevent a false exit by making the modern player think of the grouping on stage as different.[12] Because repertory work on a stage bare of scenery, then, places too heavy demands on the memory, Shakespeare relieves his principal players, as well as his supernumeraries, by presenting them with lines which in their wording are obviously exit cues. Lines of dialogue can be forgotten and prompted without great harm, en-

12. False exits done in rehearsals on a bare stage normally disappear during the first rehearsal with scenery and furniture.

trances can afford occasional delay in execution, but a
misplaced exit or a failure to exit at the proper moment can readily inflict on a play damage that is irre-
versible.

Not so obviously cues as announcements and requests are the rhyming couplets that often mark exits
in Shakespeare's plays. Since the majority of such
couplets occur along with either exit requests or announcements, they can hardly be taken as exit cues
themselves. As a matter of fact, only a small fraction—
fifty-eight of the four hundred—of the exit couplets
in Shakespeare appear unaccompanied by another
kind of cue. A typical example appears in *2 Henry VI*
(III.i.382–83) ending a soliloquy of fifty-three lines
which has no other rhyme in it. Here occurs no hint
of either a request or an announcement that the speaker, York, could possibly use as a signal to make his
exit. In the dramatist's next play, *3 Henry VI* (III.ii.
194–95), Richard ends an even longer soliloquy—
seventy-two lines—with the same type of cue, again
without request or announcement to remind him of
the exit, and again without other rhyming couplets in
the speech. The Scrivener in *Richard III* does the
same thing at the end of a soliloquy that consumes a
whole scene (III.vi.13–14), and a scene of similar
length is completely taken by Artemidorus in *Julius
Caesar,* whose only rhyme (II.iii.15–16) ends the soliloquy. In *Measure for Measure,* the dramatist has Angelo cue himself with a rhyming couplet (II.ii.186–87)
which ends a twenty-six line soliloquy otherwise in
blank verse, and Iago is made to preface his exit by
concluding a soliloquy of twenty-seven lines with a
rhyme (*Othello* II.i.320–21). All these examples of
rhyming couplets as the actor's sole cue to exit are delivered under the same circumstances: by characters
alone on stage, in soliloquy. It is equally true that the

closing rhyme gives a definitiveness to the soliloquy and the exit which they would otherwise lack, that the couplet acts as a figurative curtain to grace the exit, and that often the rhyme dramatically emphasizes the relative importance of the final two lines, making them more memorable. But the fact remains that almost every time a player in Shakespeare's dramas has only the couplet as his exit cue, he is alone, or technically alone (with a dead or sleeping character) on the stage. In only some half dozen cases is a player accompanied by conscious characters when his exit is marked by the rhyming couplet alone, without an additional announcement or request.[13] And if any of them originally ended scenes on an inner space, the closing curtain would have obviated the need for an exit cue. The paucity of exceptions would therefore seem to indicate that the dramatist intended rhyming couplets to function, among other things, as exit cues only when the players who delivered them were alone on the stage, giving soliloquies.

Equally interesting, though few in number, are instances where the dramatist seems to reinforce with a couplet another type of exit cue delivered too long ago in the performance for safety. In *The Comedy of Errors* (IV.iii.80), for illustration, Antipholus of Syracuse delivers this parting shot to the Courtesan as he leaves the stage with Dromio—"Avaunt, thou Witch"— surely an exit request. But since she herself is not supposed to exit for nearly twenty more lines, the dramatist provides her with a rhyming couplet (96-97) at the end of her lengthy soliloquy, a couplet that also ends the scene. The Bastard in *King John* is even

---

13. *Richard III,* IV.iv.195-96; *Hamlet,* III.i.195-96; *Troilus and Cressida,* V.iii.111-12; *All's Well That Ends Well,* I.iii. 261-62; *Macbeth,* V.viii.33-34; *Timon of Athens,* III.iii. 25-26.

more in need of a second cue, for he follows the King's exit request to him with a soliloquy extending to thirty-seven lines. Shakespeare gives it to him, in the form of a concluding rhyme (II.i.597–98), to remind him to leave the stage. And in two cases,[14] at least, soliloquists are made to reinforce their own exit announcements with rhyming couplets at the end of long monologues.

Now it may be argued that these delayed exits (along with some others in the plays) invalidate requests and announcements as cues, but this is not at all the case. If a player has memorized a soliloquy that he is to deliver after an exit announcement or request, he will tend to disregard it temporarily as a cue. Anyway, in the instances cited even if the actor sacrificed the soliloquy to obey the exit cue at once, very little damage would be done. None of the soliloquies referred to above is as important to the play as the exit. In fact, really vital soliloquies never seem to occur after exit cues which might cancel their delivery. One thing is certain: to consider any requests or announcements as exit cues, we must assume all of them to be such. To expect actors in repertory to discriminate between requests and announcements that are cues and those that are not would be self-defeating and more damaging than omitting exit cues altogether. The same, of course, applies to rhyming couplets as exit cues. A player cannot be expected to distinguish between rhymes that are cues and rhymes that are not. Especially in Shakespeare's plays is this true, where the overwhelming majority of rhyming couplets (eight hundred of the twelve hundred) actually do not occur at places where there are supposed to be exits. On the

14. *Richard III,* I.i.147–62, and *Hamlet,* IV.iv.32–66, in a soliloquy that does not appear in the Folio text.

other hand, it would be relatively simple to train actors in exiting only on those rhymes delivered in their soliloquies. A player can reasonably be expected to be aware of the fact that he occupies the stage alone.

But what, then, can be said about rhyming couplets occurring in soliloquies given by actors who fail to exit? In *The Comedy of Errors,* for instance, Antipholus of Syracuse definitely ends his nine-line soliloquy with a rhyme (III.ii.168–69)—

> But, let myself be guilty to self-wrong,
> I'll stop mine ears against the mermaid's
>   song

yet he does not leave the stage. The explanation for his unusual behavior appears in what immediately follows: first, there is the notation in the Folio, *"Enter Angelo with the chain,"* then, a brief exchange between the two men:

> *Angelo.* Master Antipholus!
> *Antipholus.* Ay, that's my name.

What happens, then, is evident: Antipholus does take his rhyme as a cue to exit, but he is prevented from leaving the stage by Angelo. The method that prevents Richard III from following the rhyming cue in his soliloquy (*Richard III,* I.i.38–41) with an exit is possibly even clearer—

> This day should Clarence closely be mew'd up
> About a prophecy which says that G
> Of Edward's heirs the murtherer be.
> Dive, thoughts, down to my soul! Here Clar-
>   ence comes,

because, it will be noticed, he actually makes the announcement of his brother's entrance immediately after his exit couplet. And at least seven other enterers

in the plays evidently prevent exits cued by rhymes
from materializing.[15]

Couplets of a somewhat different character delivered by soliloquists who fail to carry out their exit
also sometimes appear in the plays. In a soliloquy of
thirty-five lines, for instance, Richard III emits a
rhyme at about the middle of his speech (*Richard III,*
I.ii.239–40)—

> Hath she forgot already that brave prince,
> Edward her lord, whom I, some three months
> since . . .

—but this is obviously what may be called an open
couplet, which may be regarded as accidental rather
than designed as an exit cue. No actor, surely, would
be tempted to exit (or even to pause verbally) in the
middle of a sentence. Probably he would fail even to
notice such a rhyme. The dramatist permits Henry IV
to slip into a similar rhyme in the early portion of the
familiar apostrophe to sleep (*2 Henry IV*, III.i.12–13),
which the actor delivers while alone on stage. In a
much later play, *Timon of Athens,* one of the senators
falls into rhyme during his soliloquy concerning the
hero:

> —why, give my horse to Timon.
> Ask nothing, give it to him—it foals me
> straight,
> And able horses. No porter at his gate . . .
> (II.i.8–10)

which continues with the words, "But rather one that
smiles. . . ." Here again the rhyming word, appearing

15. *The Two Gentlemen of Verona,* I.i.68–70; *Cymbeline,*
III.v.64–66, V.iii.80–83; *Titus Andronicus,* II.iii.8–10; *Romeo
and Juliet,* II.v.16–18; *Twelfth Night,* III.i.74–76; *Measure for
Measure,* III.ii.198–200.

as it does in a new sentence, could hardly confuse the speaker, especially as it also does not end the sentence. It is apparent, then, that Shakespeare exercised extreme care not to encourage false exits by placing closed rhyming couplets in soliloquies where they did not belong. Indeed, fully fourteen of the plays give no rhyming lines whatsoever to soliloquists except at points where they are supposed to make an exit.[16] Furthermore, soliloquies minus couplets are delivered by players without exits much more frequently than soliloquies with rhyming couplets are by players with exits.[17]

More impressive, many soliloquies without couplets are of imposing length, long enough to allow a dramatist who was not consciously avoiding rhymes to slip some in. In *Henry V,* for example, the King extends a soliloquy to fifty-five lines without including a rhyming couplet, either open or closed, accidental or intentional. The most famous of soliloquists, Hamlet, delivers a monologue of twenty-one lines without rhyming. Angelo, in *Measure for Measure,* begins a scene with a rhymeless soliloquy of seventeen lines, and Edmund, in *King Lear,* opens another with a blank verse soliloquy that extends to twenty-two lines. Timon is given to present a long soliloquy of forty-seven lines without once being permitted to slip into a rhyming couplet. And in *Cymbeline,* Posthumus avoids rhyme in a soliloquy that consumes a whole scene. But the

16. *1 Henry VI, The Taming of the Shrew, Richard II, The Merchant of Venice, 1 Henry IV, Much Ado About Nothing, Henry V, As You Like It, Hamlet, The Merry Wives of Windsor, King Lear, Coriolanus, The Winter's Tale,* and *The Tempest.*

17. Approximately 225 soliloquies contain no rhyming couplets whatever. Of these, nearly 150 are in verse, where we should expect rhymes to slip in more easily than in prose soliloquies. In contrast, only about fifty soliloquies contain bona fide exit couplets.

Shakespearean character most careful about uttering rhyming couplets in the wrong place is Richard II, who is made to keep them out of a monologue extending to sixty-six lines, his only pure soliloquy in the play. Yet in dialogue between two or more characters, couplets where there is no call for an exit are common.

The final result of a thoroughgoing search was the detection of only eight[18] of the nearly 2,000 bona fide exits in the plays without either a discernible cue or the likelihood of the inner-space curtain closing in front of the players and thereby obviating the need for one. The dearth of exceptions appears to strengthen the conclusion that the playwright, while frequently adding to the dramatic impact of the scene, consciously helped his fellow actors in repertory theater to exit from a bare stage at the proper time by giving them announcements to make, requests to obey, or (if they were to be alone on the stage at the time) rhyming couplets to remind them to depart. It is additional evidence that Shakespeare is not only a brilliant dramatist but also a master craftsman.

18. In *2 Henry VI*, I.iii.140; *Richard III*, I.iii.297–303; *Love's Labour's Lost*, IV.i.127–30; *Henry V*, IV.i.64–83; *Troilus and Cressida*, V.iv.20–26; *All's Well That Ends Well*, III.ii.20; *Cymbeline*, IV.ii.100; *The Winter's Tale*, IV.iii.462–73.

Index

Index

Index

Index

Index

Index

Index

Index

Parolles (*All's Well That Ends Well*), 50
Paulina (*Winter's Tale*), 46 n.
Peele, George: *Arraignment of Paris*, 14 n.; *David and Bethsabe*, 14 n., 75 n.; *Edward I*, 73 n.; *Old Wives Tale*, 4 n., 14 n., 73 n.
Pericles, xi
Perkin Warbeck. See Ford
Petruchio (*Taming of the Shrew*), 74
Philaster. See Beaumont and Fletcher
Pindarus (*Julius Caesar*), 42, 43
Pisanio (*Cymbeline*), 26, 63
Pistol (*2 Henry IV*), 11 n.
Platform, 4 n., 8, 15, 35 n.; outer, 5, 10 and n., 72-73; developed into modern apron, 10 n.; definitions, 35 n.; raised, conjectured existence of, 35-37
Playhouse, Elizabethan public: physical aspects to which Shakespeare adapted conventions, ix, 2, 5, 6, 79; as viewed by spectators, 14-21, 22 n.; walls, 36; appearance of, 76-77; ever-present daylight in, 83. *See also* Apron; Arras; Balcony stage; Curtains; Dais; Entranceway(s); Gallery; Globe Theatre; Inner space; Platform; Pulpit; Stage, Shakespeare's; Tiring house; Wall
Poins (*1 Henry IV*), 81
Polixenes (*Winter's Tale*), 16, 91
Pompey (*Antony and Cleopatra*), 66 and n.

Portia: (*Julius Caesar*), 73; (*Merchant of Venice*), 58
Posthumus (*Cymbeline*), 26, 61, 106
Preston, Thomas, *Cambises*, 14 n.
Prompter, 24-33, 99
Properties. *See* Stage properties
Proscenium arch, 5, 8; and entrance announcements, 4 n.
Prospero (*Tempest*), 90, 91
Proteus (*Two Gentlemen of Verona*), 5, 6, 50
Puck (*Midsummer Night's Dream*), 7, 8, 77 n.
Pulpit, 40-41, 42

Ratcliff (*Richard III*), 11 n.
Regnier (*1 Henry VI*), 38
Regrouping. *See* Shift in position onstage
Rehearsal. See Buckingham, Duke of
Repertory players, Elizabethan and modern, 99-101
Rhyming couplets: as exit cues, 101-4; marking delayed exits, 102-4; not marking exit cues, 104-6; absence of, in long soliloquies, 106-7
Richard: (*3 Henry VI*), 101; (*Richard II*), 13 n., 36-37, 62, 77, 107; (*Richard III*), 11 n., 16, 61, 104, 105
Richard II, 2 n., 10 n., 13 n., 16 and n., 36, 49 n., 50 n., 59-60, 64 n., 74 n., 75, 81 n., 92, 106 n.
Richard III, xi, 10 n., 11 n., 16, 26, 27, 28 n., 29 n., 31 n., 51 n., 61 and n.,

Index

Index

Index